Business Re-engineering

with

Information Technology

Sustaining Your Business Advantage

An Implementation Guide

John J. Donovan

P T R Prentice .
Englewood Cliffs, New Jersey 07632

Library of Congress Cataloguing-in-Publication Data

Editorial/production supervision: *Mary P. Rottino*
Cover design: *Lundgren Graphics*
Cover photo: *Letraset USA Phototone Vol. 1*
Manufacturing manager: *Alexis Heydt*
Acquisitions editor: *Paul Becker*
Editorial assistant: *Maureen Diana*

Published by P T R Prentice Hall
Prentice-Hall, Inc.
A Paramount Communications Company
Englewood Cliffs, New Jersey 07632

The publisher offers discounts on this book when ordered in bulk quantites.
For more information contact: Corporate Sales Department, P T R Prentice Hall,
113 Sylvan Ave., Englewood Cliffs, NJ 07632.
Phone (201) 592-2863   Fax (201) 592-2249

Printed in the United States of America

10 9 8 7 6 5 4

ISBN 0-13-311028-1

Prentice-Hall International (UK) Limited, *London*
Prentice-Hall of Australia Pty. Limited, *Sydney*
Prentice-Hall Canada Inc., *Toronto*
Prentice-Hall Hispanoamericana, S.A., *Mexico*
Prentice-Hall of India Private Limited, *New Delhi*
Prentice-Hall of Japan, Inc., *Tokyo*
Simon & Schuster Asia Pte. Ltd., *Singapore*
Editora Prentice-Hall do Brasil, Ltda., *Rio de Janeiro*

Life is a verb, not a noun.

Buckminster Fuller

Contents

Preface

This book is based on interactions with more than 600 CEOs in 1994, and more than 3,000 executives from over 1,000 corporations. The insights that each of these men and women have given make them all, in the truest sense of the word, authors of this book.

For you, the reader, this book presents a road map in your journey to add value to your organization's products and services through technology. It is not the road map one finds in the three dozen books per year on how to make a million in something or other.

Rather, this book offers a substantial strategy through which your organization will be able to respond to urgent business demands with the speed necessary to maintain a competitive advantage in a dynamic, global economy.

This is an executive handbook for identifying and implementing strategic applications using information technology.

The approach described here enables you and your organization to modernize your information technology infrastructure in order to sustain a competitive advantage in today's dynamic environment.

How This Book Works

This book shows you a business and information technology (IT) strategy that *works*, a strategy built on a system architecture that is robust, flexible, and specifically designed for the dynamics of today's winning businesses. It is an architecture that is already helping more than 3,000 of the world's most successful organizations get the most from their information systems. And best of all, it is an architecture that puts *you* back in control through its *vendor independence.* You decide which hardware and software components best fit your requirements, regardless of which vendor provides them. You can mix and match products and regain maximum leverage of your existing in-house systems and processes. *Your business is in harmony with your information technology!*

The best testament to vendor independence is the campaign by major hardware and systems makers to promote vendor independence. The campaign must be an anathema to sales forces everywhere. But top marketing strategists in the computer industry know the truth: The only way that they can hold onto existing customers is by promoting open solutions—and even, at times, forthrightly suggesting that a customer use a product from a competing computer company.

To focus on the business principles, we will examine actual businesses throughout the book. In Chapter 1, we discuss the foundations of today's global business environment and explore the opportunities facing organizations everywhere. In Chapter 2, we explore the "common sense" business strategies that so many organizations employ to resolve their crises—and reveal why such "solutions" are actually prescriptions for failure.

The key to success is identifying and continually implementing strategic applications that produce added value. Chapter 3 presents cases that illustrate successful uses of the client-server architecture, the cornerstone of an information technology strategy that harmonizes your business with IT.

Chapter 4 lays out a business description of an implementation process that works. It gives you a structured process for finding strategic business applications, including identification of strategic applications, empowerment for existing MIS organizations, and exploitation of "hidden treasures." These are valued business opportunities that emerge unexpectedly from the firm foundation of your new information architecture.

Chapter 5 provides a framework for the business determination of your IT options. Here is the IT strategy blueprint.

In Chapter 6, we present the business enabling characteristics of the new 3-tiered client-server architecture, and describe the tools available to implement this architecture today. Although this book is *not* a technical treatise, we do provide a technical overview to substantiate our claim for this information technology architecture.

Chapters 7 and 8 lay out a specific IT implementation process for achieving tangible results within your organization *in 20 weeks or less*. Imagine gaining strategic business advantage over your competitors in so short a time! These chapters show you how, by creating a functional pilot system within three weeks, and then extending it into an industrial-strength production system in 10-20 weeks.

Chapter 9 discusses strategies for dealing with the dramatic changes that client-server architecture brings to the role of the Chief Information Officer and to relationships with your technology vendors. Finally, Chapters 10 and 11 look ahead, pondering the strategic implications of emerging trends on the technology horizon. What tools will be available that your organization should be positioning itself to exploit? We give you a few intriguing ideas.

Appendix A gives a more technical presentation of the software tools needed to build applications in a 3-tiered client-server architecture.

Appendix B provides guidance on resisting the siren call of those within and beyond your organization who would hold you back from realizing your vision, or who would wreck your strategy on the rocks of a proprietary, 2-tiered approach or other traditional environments. Beware their lure.

Each chapter begins with a summary of its major points and concludes, when appropriate, with a to-do list of specific first steps.

As economic power declines, ideological power follows. The standard of living in a region is directly related to its productivity. We will all have succeeded if the methods in this book help you to increase your organization's productivity and to support its ability to meet its higher purpose, fulfilling a social responsibility.

Our goal is to put a new business weapon in your hands, or at least modernize one already in your arsenal. A 3-tiered client-server architecture using open systems based on Open Distributed Environment tools can deliver a powerful advantage over your opponents. But remember: The effectiveness of any weapon is limited by the skill and determination of the one who wields it. Let the training begin.

On a personal note, as an executive reading this book, I want you to know that I realize that your job is much harder than mine. You must implement what I describe. My best to you.

Acknowledgments

This book builds upon 12 years of contributions and experiences of the executives that have attended programs at Cambridge Technology Group (CTGroup), all of CTGroup's employees, and the employees of Open Environment Corporation (OEC), Object Power, and Migration Strategies. One result of that decade-plus of experience is the 3-tiered client-server architecture described on the following pages. The architecture was introduced by CTGroup and later adopted by the industry as a fundamental model of a robust client-server architecture.

This book in particular reflects the creative output of a very special relationship with Sundar Subramaniam and the support of the following people: Adam Honig, Alex Shah, Charles Stefanidakis, Danny Kim, Frank Sena, Greg Kelton, Ron Downs, Michael Lee, Jim Nondorf, Kathryn Walker, Terry Wise, Marco Lara, Maureen Lantz, Melanie Thistle, Michael Fan, Suzanne Rheault, Swapnil Shah, Tony Salas, Alan Lehotsky, Rom Sudama, and John Donovan IV.

Special acknowledgment is given to Paul MacAvoy, Dean of the Yale School of Organization and Management for his enduring friendship, insight, and hard work.

In addition, thanks to Joseph T. Jaynes, president of Synaptic Systems Corporation, Dani Danzig, Bill Gruener, Alan Southerton, and Judith Tarutz for assistance in editing this book.

I also wish to acknowledge my children for their support.

Cambridge, Massachusetts John J. Donovan
February 1994

Manufactured in the United States of America.

Other books by Professor Donovan:
Systems Programming (1972)
Operating Systems (1974)
Software Projects (1985)
Crisis in Technology (1990)
Opportunities in Technology (1991)
Business &Technology: A Paradigm Shift (1992)
Business Re-engineering with Technology (1993)

xviii

About the Author

Professor John J. Donovan is Chairman, Cambridge Technology Group and Adjunct Professor, MIT. Other companies founded by Professor Donovan include Open Environment Corporation and recently

 Migration Strategies and Object Power. Dr. Donovan has received his Ph.D. from Yale and was a tenured member of the faculty of the Massachusetts Institute of Technology, first in Electrical Engineering and then in Management. He was Assistant Clinical Professor of Pediatrics at Tufts Medical School and a lecturer at Harvard University, and continues to serve as an Adjunct Professor of Management at MIT's Sloan School of Management. In government, Professor Donovan is a member of the Department of Defense's Information Systems Advisory Council. He pioneered the basis for compiler design, Multics, VM interprocess communications, and the 3-tiered computing architecture. Dr. Donovan is the author of seven books, including *Systems Programming, Operating Systems,* and most recently, *Business and Technology: A Paradigm Shift*, each of which has been translated into nine languages.

Dr. Donovan is the father of five wonderful children. He enjoys farming, horseback riding, home renovation, and boating with his family.

The Bottom Line

The bottom line for organizations everywhere is confusing—although there are tremendous opportunities, organizations are struggling. The business questions are the same, but the old strategies are not working.

When a student told Professor Einstein, "These are the same questions as on last year's test," the professor responded, "Oh yes, but the answers are different this year."

What are today's business answers, what are the information technology (IT) strategies that will work?

Executives and leaders are frustrated. Business processes and information technology are not in harmony. Yet information technology remains a major hope for adding value to products and services. What is going on?

Organizations Face Crisis/Opportunity

The Chinese ideographs for "crisis" and "opportunity" are the same! All over the world today, many organizations (businesses, governments, non-profit groups) are struggling while others prosper. Change is everywhere, but it is the rate of change that has changed. It has speeded up.

- Taiwan deregulated its insurance and banking industries this year and went from six major banks to

18. Yet those industries have had trouble implementing the needed IT changes so that they could respond to a shift in mortgage terms from 20 years to 30.

- Today, 14,000 American banks exist. Consolidation is occurring, but IT is not helping.

- In 1994, Sears Roebuck will lay off 50,000 employees, close 100 stores, and sell its insurance and real estate units.

- Another retailer, Walmart, will buy 214 stores and become the 6th most valuable organization in the world, with $75 billion in market capitalization. That's enough to buy IBM and GM together!

- Walmart had an IT and business strategy that allowed for growth in a dynamic, fast-changing business, using IT effectively in areas such as supplier relations and inventory. Sears did not.

- In the first 70 years of their history (1920-1990), U.S. airlines generated $3.8 billion in profits. During the most recent 18 months, they lost $4.8 billion.

- Singapore Airlines remains profitable.

- Swissair, British Air, Scandinavian Airlines, KLM Royal Dutch Airlines, Austrian and other European airlines have taken drastic measures in an attempt to stem their losses.

- Phillips Electronics fell 170 positions in ranking of market capitalization in the past 12 months and has adapted a strategy of selling its video unit and laying off people.

Many organizations are attempting to address the swiftly changing business climate by adopting barriers to entry through relatively static, easily replicated business strategies such as:

- Cost cutting
- Protectionism
- Financial restructuring
- Brand name identification

These are coupled with relatively slow IT strategies of traditional:

- Data modeling
- Life cycle development
- Mainframe, centralized development
- Proprietary tools

While such tactics may provide short-term relief, they are actually prescriptions for today's failure. Although they may satisfy short-term needs for survival, they do not provide a foundation for a successful long-term strategy.

What will work? Simply put:

Organizations thrive only by continuously adding value to their products and services (e.g., faster time to market, continuously higher quality, ease of doing business, etc.), coupled with an IT strategy that is adaptable, open, 3-tiered, and standards-based.

IT Is the Key to Today's Added Value

In today's business environment, the major tool to add value or, in some cases, a major component of the added value is the *information*. Yet when we asked the hundreds of CEOs who have visited CTGroup over the past few years how well their information technology (IT) has served them, they nearly unanimously replied,

"IT is a disaster!"

"IT is my *inhibitor*, not my enabler!"

Here are a few examples of their frustrations. For a bank to add value to its products and services, it must focus on its customers. But how are the computer systems of every bank on the planet organized? *By product—not by customer.* That is, you go into one product system to find a person's checking account information, another product computer for private banking, another for mortgage information, and so forth. You cannot enter one name and find all the banking relationships for that customer.

Furthermore, the business situation that has dictated bank consolidation is not in harmony with the information technology systems that must be assimilated. The former president of Security Pacific Bank (at that time the 4th largest bank in the U.S.) reported that he had difficulty knowing exactly how much money he had in his own bank! Every time he acquired a new bank, he got another incompatible general ledger.

Business processes are interconnected, but information technologies are not. Two insurance organizations visiting CTGroup this year reported that the claims systems and premium systems were not connected. The result? Claims were paid to customers who had not paid their premiums, as was the case this year with Blue Cross of New York.

Manufacturing organizations have computer systems organized *by function—not by process.* Today, IBM, Digital Equipment Corporation, and Hewlett Packard are unable to assist their sales staff in the selling or ordering process by giving them a complete, on-line profile of a customer, listing equipment on order, installed configuration, service history, sales history, or payment history. There is a separate function system for each portion of this information

Another way to state the problem is *that IT is not in harmony with the business.* Does this sound like your business?

Harmony Is the Answer

What can you do? The answer is twofold: develop a business strategy and develop an IT strategy.

- *Develop a business strategy.* Recognize that the details of implementation will constantly change in response to variables such as deregulation, regulation, phases of competition, globalization, new opportunities, technological changes, diversification, consolidation, and focus.

- *Develop an IT strategy.* Recognize that it must swiftly accommodate changes in two dimensions: technological changes (multimedia, objects, the dramatic reduction in the cost of hardware) and the business changes that IT must support.

CEOs, users, and MIS staff must regard information systems in the same way as other business tools. Are you ever finished with the project of improving your quality? Your profit? Of course not—and your information technology projects will never be finished either. Information systems will have functionality delivered within weeks, but they will continue to evolve to *harmonize* with ever-changing business needs.

This book explains the mechanisms for achieving the harmony that your organization so desperately needs. We will give you a different focus for your business: to add value continuously. We will give you a different architecture for your information technology: a 3-tiered client-server architecture based on an Open Distributed Environment , ODE.

What is special about open systems? Technological considerations aside, the key ingredient to open systems is that it lets you decide the direction of your information technology. It provides the pieces to the information technology puzzle and allows you to assemble and change them quickly. And with 3-tiered client-server architecture, the puzzle is not a puzzle at all: It is your picture of IT growth and capitalization. And most important, we will give you a new realization:

Business—and the information technology that empowers it—is a journey, not a destination. Your job is to guide your organization along that journey.

Business Situations

In 1850, the German armorer Krupp tried in vain to convince the French to use his radical new steel cannon instead of bronze. When the Franco-Prussian war broke out in 1870, the Prussians, using Krupp's cannon, crushed the French army. The new cannon provided twice the range and twice the firepower of the old cannons [*The Arms of Krupp*, 1990].

The new cannon today is the IT architecture discussed here. What has happened in IT since 1990? Here's a preview: a drop in hardware cost by a factor of 1,000 (not just the two that crushed the French army) and an agreement (never reached before in the computer industry) in 1994 to standardize how programs talk to each other and the articulation of the 3-tiered architecture. But let's move along and return to these IT advances later.

This decade presents stunning business opportunities: Organizations are spanning the globe; new markets are opening in China and Eastern Europe; banks are freed to enter new businesses; manufacturers are integrating their operations with suppliers and distributors; old political systems are crumbling and, with them, old obstacles to international trade. And the list goes on.

For corporations not interested in expanding abroad, the opportunities are no less significant. Thanks to technological innovation in our own infrastructure—detailed tracking of existing customer databases, on-line services, and opportunities to redeploy resources and begin new ventures in areas such as credit and communications—no corporation is without opportunity in this exciting decade.

You see it everywhere you look. Upheaval. Turmoil. The rapid metamorphosis of traditional modes of thought and ways of doing business into radically new paradigms.

Is your organization prepared to exploit the new opportunities presented by this tidal wave of change? Or are you straining to hold back the flood—to stem the tide of change in the hope that tomorrow will be more like yesterday?

The tide is irresistible. You must learn to swim—and learn quickly—or risk having your business swept away.

Urgency—Revolution Is Required

Our mission in this book is to revolutionize the way that you do business, and to support that revolution with a constantly evolving information technology. This is the heart of our message:

Your business must constantly adapt to a dynamically changing environment. Therefore you must choose an adaptive, dynamic information architecture that has the flexibility to support both changes in the business environment and changes in technology.

The ability to identify and apply the appropriate computing and communications options will determine which organizations succeed in the next decade. We already see organizations facing difficulties because of competition, government, internal forces, and the need for an appropriate business strategy and information technology infrastructure. For example:

- In 1994, U.S. banks own less than 8% of the world's banking assets. In 1960, they owned over 61%. What business strategy and IT strategy will help given their difficult climate?

- Today, banks face a five-tiered regulatory system, while other financial institutions from American Express to Fidelity to General Motors have been able to compete with similar services nationally (e.g., you can write a check on your Fidelity account).

To further exacerbate the situation, IT infrastructures in most banks do not facilitate fast, new product releases, customer focus, risk analysis, or consolidation. For example, the Bank of New England lost over $2 billion in 1990, yet their information architecture prevented them from determining the total risk exposure for their clients.

The right business strategy coupled with the wrong IT strategy is a disaster. Here are two examples:

- In 1993, the London Stock Exchange abandoned "Taurus," the computerized settlement system that would have allowed them to be a global competitor. Development costs ran £400 million over a six-year period.

- In 1982, the U.S. air traffic control system seemed to be on the verge of collapse. A new computer system was announced, to be delivered in 1992. In 1993, the FAA's Advanced Automation System (AAS) is still nine years from completion and, at a total cost of $5.1 billion, is $1.5 billion over budget.

"But," you say, "I've heard this all before. Every computer vendor I talk to tells me his latest hardware and software will 'revolutionize' my business. That's what got me into the mess I'm in!"

You're right. The strategies promoted in the past by hardware vendors have *not* fulfilled the promise of business empowerment and strategic advantage. *Those strategies are fundamentally flawed* when confronted with today's business realities. The old strategies emerged to solve problems that no longer exist, and they are unable to evolve rapidly enough to deal with the real-world problems that face you today.

1

Today's Reality:
Organizations in Crisis

"No company is safe . . . there is no such
thing as a 'solid,' or even substantial, lead over
one's competitors. Too much is changing for
anyone to be complacent. Moreover, the 'champ
to chump' cycles are growing ever shorter . . ."

Tom Peters, *Thriving on Chaos*

"[Blue Cross's] new computer system,
dubbed System 21 because it is supposed to carry
the company into the 21st century, is behind
schedule and tens of millions of dollars over
budget. System 21's original budget was less than
$100 million, but Blue Cross has already spent
$80 million and estimates the final bill at $166
million . . . The president quits after loss of one
million customers out of three million. Blue
Cross is asking for a 48% group increase, but the
computer system is still not processing claims
correctly."

The Boston Globe, 1994.

Executive Summary

The common thread that runs through the previous excerpts is that business is changing and traditional IT is not supporting these changes. In all cases when the consumer, whether a large corporation or an individual, is willing to pay for a service, information technology should guarantee that this is the only toll levied against the consumer. In other words, the technology infrastructure of a company should place little, if any, burden on the consumer. From insurance claims to on-line manuals for jet fighter aircraft, the consumer doesn't want to be involved in the underlying technology infrastructure. The consumer wants to press a button or seal an envelope. Nothing more.

That consumers are beginning to recognize the benefits of open systems technology puts the steel edge to the radical transformation occurring in the modern marketplace. Organizations that continue to operate using the expectations and models of the old business environment are struggling to survive:

- Traditional business relationships and operational models are evolving or collapsing.

- New opportunities exist for businesses that can use information technology to create and capitalize on emerging markets.

- Market expectations and pressures are changing.

- Global business opportunities are expanding (and information technology is crucial to realizing and managing these opportunities).

A World Turned Upside Down

The business world confronting you today is a different place from the one you knew a decade ago. Companies long thought to be invincible (American Express, Phillips, Nissan, Daimler Benz, IBM, Eastman Kodak, General Motors, Sears Roebuck, and others) are suddenly struggling to survive. Consider this example:

- In the 1970s, the major consumer product suppliers (Proctor and Gamble, Johnson & Johnson, Unilever) dictated product terms to the retailers. By 1994, a retailer (Walmart) ranked 6th in the world in market value, and dictated terms to consumer product suppliers, outsourcing its inventory, advertising, and shelf management to them.

What is going on in business today? Why are some thriving and others struggling? And what role does information technology play in those failures and successes? These are the key questions you must answer for your business to thrive in the new global marketplace.

First, let's examine the traits that characterize this new environment.

Business Opportunities Are Expanding

Information technology has two important roles to play as business opportunities re-ignite after the chaotic 1980s. In international business, information technology obviates old concerns such as physical distance, the safety of employees abroad, and the usually high initial capitalization required. At home, advances in information technology allow astute corporations entry into

13

new markets. In both arenas, IT allows for a dramatic, continuous improvement of quality, customer focus, speed to market, and product improvement.

Businesses today have another new reality that they must deal with: The constantly changing global political/economic partnership. Recent key events tell the story:

- The passage by the European Economic Community of GATT.

- In North America, the acceptance of NAFTA by the USA, Candada, and Mexico.

- Asia's APEC.

- The reacquisition of Hong Kong by China, plus the growth of its stock market. China's vast population of 1.4 billion and its economic growth rated 13% over the last decade, all indicating economic possibilities.

- The fall of the Iron Curtain. This event promises to eventually create new markets in the former states of the Soviet Union.

These are all global opportunities that can open up markets. And organizations that use the capabilities of a 3-tiered, open computing environment can seize these opportunities.

All in all, new market opportunities must be met with focused, culturally targeted, correct, high-growth products and services.

Privatization, Regulation, Deregulation, and Globalization

The 1990s, characterized by rapid business change, privatization in Russia and Eastern Europe, spreading capitalism in China, and widespread governmental deregulation in the U.S., generated tremendous changes in many traditional businesses throughout the world.

Airlines and transportation, telecommunications and data networking, banking and finance—industries once tightly controlled and managed—suddenly discovered that all the rules had changed. Former technological barriers to entry disappeared. Companies like MCI and Sprint could challenge giants like AT&T because of the exponential drop in prices and increases in capacity of computers and data transmission networks. Banks and insurance companies could never have offered the vast new array of services and products now available without an adequate and affordable computing and networking infrastructure.

These changes create a large and constantly churning pool of new markets and business opportunities waiting to be captured by organizations with sufficient flexibility and vision.

Expanded International Markets

The political transformation of Eastern Europe and China, the rapid industrialization of the Far East and Latin America, the growing economic unification of the Common Market countries—factors such as these herald the appearance of markets that did not exist a mere decade ago. These markets hold vast potential for growth, but present unique challenges that many organizations are ill-equipped to meet. Products and services must be adapted to the culture and language requirements of each country. Marketing and distribution functions must accommodate local expectations and realities.

Businesses and IT Are Not Synchronized

While organizations ponder the new opportunities that emerging markets offer, they must also contend with rapid transformations in traditional business relationships. They must contend with new operating models in areas such as mergers and acquisitions, downsizing and layoffs, and supplier-vendor-customer relationships.

Mergers and Acquisitions

The expansion of working capital provided by the growth of the last decade has led many companies to try to broaden market share through mergers and buyouts. When mergers occur, opportunities arise to take advantage of merged product lines, inventory, purchasing, and financial analysis to provide a unified presentation to customers. Unfortunately, incompatibilities among corporate cultures, processes, and business practices, and among information systems often impede this opportunity.

Downsizing and Layoffs

Rather than expanding their holdings, other organizations have sought to refocus their efforts on their "core business" functions. Such a focus has led to widespread restructuring, downsizing, and personnel reductions as business functions are consolidated and streamlined. Unfortunately, "streamlined" processes are usually difficult to achieve, since the outmoded information systems that support them cannot be quickly and easily changed to meet the new business requirements. The actual result is fewer people trying to do the same old jobs with the same cumbersome tools. You know what this situation leads to: dissatisfaction, low morale, and increased attrition among those employees most critical to the organization's long-term survival. It might be more appropriate to call this strategy "dumbsizing."

Supplier-Vendor-Customer Relationships

Perhaps most unsettling of all, the relationships that companies have long had with their suppliers and customers, carefully nurtured through repeated cycles of growth and decline, have suddenly become outmoded. Consider these examples:

- Proctor and Gamble and other suppliers must contend with a customer like Walmart, which requires its *vendors* to manage inventory and shelf space within its own stores! This new relationship requires a partnership to be crafted between suppliers and their customers.

- A global consumer products organization like Unilever must focus on the entire supply chain, linking its information systems to suppliers, manufacturers, and customers. Yet many of the supply chain's components keep changing.

- Insurance firms must integrate their information systems with those of their customers (hospitals, clinics, and doctors' offices) to offer effortless statistical reporting to state and federal health agencies.

Yet in all of these cases, the inability to link computing systems inhibits the business functions of these organizations!

Market Expectations Are Changing

Finally, all organizations must respond to significant changes in the expectations and realities of the global marketplace. Most prominent are the issues of quality, time to market, and profit potentials.

Quality Expectations

Customers everywhere now expect *total* quality from an organization's products and services.

A social worker for the state of New Hampshire needs all information about his or her clients, such as food stamp eligibility, education benefits, and welfare payments. A justice worker in the state of Utah needs to know the complete criminal record of a person under arrest. In both cases, the citizens of these states need better service, even if the necessary information resides in many incompatible computer systems!

Think about your expectations of your financial institution and investment counselor. When you call them on the telephone, you expect them to be able to respond to your questions about any aspect of your account instantaneously, with perfect accuracy. You don't care whether the real estate department functions separately from stocks and bonds, in different regions of the country, on different computer systems. You want the status of your investment position *now*. And if your current provider cannot meet those customer service expectations, you will transfer your account to a firm that can.

Think about your quality expectations of the company that manufactures the aircraft carrying you from New York to Paris. Think of the company that makes the analytical equipment that certifies that the blood provided for your child's emergency surgery is pure. You expect—indeed, *demand*—perfection from those companies.

And more and more, your customers expect the same level of performance from you and your organization. Can your firm afford to be like the following?

- An organization with concerns about product quality has to record equipment faults in seven separate, incompatible systems.

- A regional Bell operating company is angering customers and facing regulatory action over an error rate as high as 23% in bills to long-distance carriers.

- An insurance company is losing business due to its 15-day lag in processing automobile insurance applications.

Time-to-Market Pressures

The organizations that can detect a market opportunity, implement a solution, and deliver it quickly are the organizations that will win!

19

There are three major considerations here:

- Bringing products and services to market quickly and efficiently, without sacrificing quality
- Recognizing instantaneous market opportunities that are created as the result of a social or political phenomenon
- Adjusting to negative geopolitical events and implementing immediate solutions for the organization's own infrastructure as well as for its customers

Profit Margin Pressures

You must improve your products and processes with less money than before, because of the pressure on profit margins. The costs of continuing to do business with current systems and processes do not keep pace. You *must* find a solution that makes your business proposition a viable and prosperous one.

Finding the right solutions involves a panoply of options. Improving the technological infrastructure is only one piece of the pie. Organizations that plan on successfully entering the 21st century must tailor all business components toward achieving the competitive edge. One way to do this—and one way currently emerging as a popular method—is refining personnel resources, especially in regard to structuring departments so they are process-oriented rather than task-oriented.

Dramatic Changes in the IT Environment

While these dramatic changes in business have been increasing, so too have there been changes in your key tool—IT has been increasing dramatically as well. People inside your organization are not the only ones faced with change. Moving your information technology to a client-server architecture based on open systems has a dramatic impact on your relationships with external technology/hardware vendors as well. In particular, choosing to use non-proprietary operating systems and communications systems gives you the freedom to select systems with the best technologies, prices, and performance characteristics from a wide variety of vendors. Proprietary systems give vendors control over you. Open systems put you into a *partnership* relationship.

Managing competing vendors can reduce your computing and communications costs dramatically while increasing the quality of the services that you receive. This section gives guidelines on how to increase the quality of your vendor services and reduce the cost of your computing and communications hardware.

The Democratization of Information Technologies

Two forces are driving the buying behavior of strategic-thinking information managers:

- Rapid advances in performance and corresponding declines in the cost of information technology components

- Industry-wide movement toward standards based on open systems specifications

The first force—performance increases coupled with cost reductions—permits the cost-effective application of information components to key business problems.

A simple example of improving technology is the dramatic reduction in the price of facsimile machines. The result has been an estimated 75% increase in the number of U.S. fax messages and nearly double that increase in the international arena. In business, increased facsimile transmission means faster response times. Gaining access to the right information before your competitors gives your business the competitive edge it needs to survive.

The second force—adoption of open systems standards—permits information-component vendors to compete for market share, assuring price reductions for the buyer.

Competition gives you, the buyer, the luxury of being selective. When you issue a request for bids on an open system, more than 50 organizations are ready to respond. Such competition ensures you of constantly improving price/performance ratios. Be careful, though. To work well, this new information democracy requires a savvy MIS electorate, educated in the issues. Let's see if new technology and open systems are real, and explore how to vote smart with this new freedom of choice.

Tumbling Prices, Soaring Performance

Let's focus on computing hardware. Consider this statement: "The price/performance ratios of computing and communications systems have improved by a factor of 1,000." Over what period of time did this improvement occur? 50 years? 30 years? 20 years? (Many pessimists might respond, "Not yet!")

The answer is less than 12 years, as illustrated by the following chart.

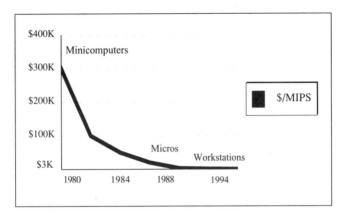

This chart plots the improvement in the price/performance of computing from 1980 through 1994, in dollars/millions of instructions per second ($/MIPS). In 1980, a typical 32-bit multi-user minicomputer cost roughly $300,000 and delivered about 1 MIPS, or $300K/MIPS. By 1988, a 32-bit multi-user microcomputer, based on the Intel 80386 CPU cost roughly $12,000 and delivered about 4 MIPS, or $3K/MIPS (a 100:1 improvement since 1980). By 1994, workstations from DEC, HP, and IBM brought the MIPS per dollar ratio down to $40 to $75 per MIP. In addition, with its strategy of concentrating on multiprocessing servers, Sun Microsystems fell into the same range—depending on how benchmarkers evaluate multiprocessing servers.

Price/performance improvements of this magnitude encourage computing to decentralize. Local systems can grow in smaller increments than in the era of mainframes, and thus respond to business requirements more effectively.

Some readers might object that this is not exactly an apples-to-apples comparison. For example, the 1980 minicomputer had more expansion capability in the number of user ports and disk storage than the 80386-based microcomputer of 1990. However, these differences are already small and, with advances in technology, are rapidly diminishing. A user running the same application on a 1980 minicomputer and a 1994 workstation will experience a price/performance improvement of about 2,000:1.

Now consider the data in the following chart.

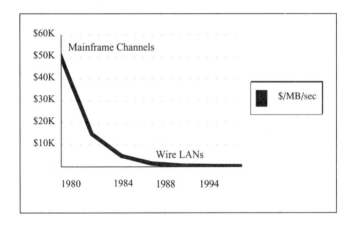

This chart plots the improvements in price/performance of local-area computer communications. The price/performance measurement here is dollars/millions of bits per second ($/MB/sec). In 1980, the only practical local area networks (LANs) were channel-based connections tying mainframes together. Typical systems delivered data at about 1 MB/sec and were priced around $50,000 for each computer connection. In 1988, twisted pair or "wire" LANs became available (adhering to standards such as IEEE 802.3), and delivered data at 1 MB/sec for about $500 per connection. The improvement in price/performance is 100:1.

One obvious impact of this price/performance improvement is the increasing cost-effectiveness of connecting PCs. Eight years ago, only a mainframe environment could justify the cost of communicating with its peers.

What's driving the price/performance curve? It is the silicon-based microprocessor. We already see chips capable of delivering 1,000 MIPS entering the marketplace.

Moreover, the pace of price/performance improvements is quickening. While the price/performance ratio exceeded 1,000:1 over the last eight years, it is not outrageous to predict that it will repeat that performance in the next 4 years. These improvements in technology have made PCs and facsimile machines ubiquitous. How many businesses have revamped their operations to leverage this diffusion of sophisticated computing and communications capability across their customer base? Very few. Business plans have traditionally assumed steady, incremental improvements in technology rather than revolutionary improvements on the order of 1,000:1.

Ten years ago, would you have permitted your strategic planners to use the following business assumption: "Computing and communications hardware costs will be zero."?

Certainly not. But you should have. Relative to all of your other costs of operation (which have undoubtedly risen), negligible computing costs would have been the right assumption. Making that assumption would have forced you to consider how changes in these technologies could affect your operations. The good news is that you get another chance. The winds of change have not stopped blowing.

Important Open Systems Standards

Businesses that are committed to gaining strategic advantage through information technology must keep a close watch on the following technologies and related industry standards.

Open Systems Standards

Technology	Relevant Standards
Computers	DCE, DME, AES, CORBA
LANs	IEEE 802.3, 802.4, 802.5
LAN Protocols	TCP/IP, ISO, X.25
PBXs, Centrex	ISDN
Telephony/WAN Interconnect	T1 circuit (de facto)
Toll-free voice/data	800 service (de facto)

These technologies are *open* as well as *standard*, which is an important distinction. Open standards are set or developed by vendor-independent bodies, chartered to meet the technological needs of the marketplace while permitting as many vendors as possible to compete. Some components, like T1 circuits for telephony and wide-area networking, appeared as proprietary, but they have become *de facto* standards with the publication of their interface specifications. Such publication allows many vendors to design compatible products. Will these de facto standards be adopted by the

26

information vendors? Yes, because customers are insisting on the freedom to choose among technology vendors that adhere to these standards.

The standards listed above are rapidly penetrating the product lines of all computing and communications vendors, as demonstrated by the popularity of ISDN, DCE (Distributed Computer Environment), and open systems. Digital switch vendors offering both PBX and central office services are pitching ISDN capabilities in their product lines. Similarly, a number of recent surveys and market studies indicate that every major computer vendor is now offering an open systems product line, including DCE. Open systems will command a 50% market share of computer systems shipped in 1995 and beyond.

Clearly, open systems standards are becoming a dominant force in the market. If your MIS department exploits these standards successfully, it can achieve dramatic improvements in price/performance and can therefore reduce operating costs. Selecting open systems also requires major changes in the way your employees relate to technology vendors.

The Old Way

The decision-making process for purchasing information hardware components used to look like this:

(see figure on p. 28)

The only time anyone had any semblance of vendor choice under the old purchasing model occurred with

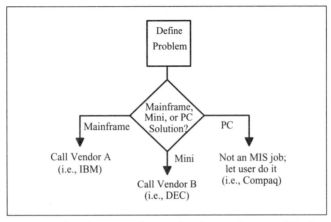

PCs once the clone vendors gained prominence. Ironically, PC choices have recently been pulled back toward a centralized decision-making model as the need to connect PCs with the rest of the corporate computing structure grew.

The New Way

More recently, real freedom of choice has returned to the vendor-selection process with the emergence of open systems. PCs and workstations can communicate with minicomputers and mainframes via DCE software and standard communications protocols. Although such communications are unlikely to alter the nature of the data that resides on the corporate mainframes, the client-server architecture allows organizations to treat the mainframe as a giant file server. Mission-critical computing can be distributed among more cost-effective workstations and PCs whose operations are based on standards.

In a few years, MIS decision-making has been transformed from a state of limited choices to a state of considerable freedom—and the number of choices continues to grow. The good news is that the increased competition created by open systems standards allows you to achieve the best value for your information dollar.

Conclusion

The realities of today's business environment are challenging indeed. So challenging, in fact, that many organizations fail to meet them. New opportunities, new relationships, and new market expectations demand new strategies for success. Only a few organizations are currently able to claim that they possess such strategies.

Is your organization one of them? If not, how can you recapture a winning posture? If your organization is successful, how can you continue!

Are there new tools that you should be aware of? For example, rapid, dramatic changes in IT include cost-performance improvements of 2000 to 1 in a ten-year period.

What business strategy should you follow? Chapter 2 examines four "common sense" business strategies to the problems of today's realities—and warns that they are more often a prescription for failure. In Chapter 5 we return to the IT strategy that will work for you.

2

"Common Sense" Solutions: Prescription for Failure

"The wrong strategy, brilliantly executed, will result in failure. A clear strategy is essential to compete effectively."

Robert Palmer, President and CEO
Digital Equipment Corporation

- *Strategy of cost cutting*: Germany's Volkswagen lays off 20,000 workers.
  Financial Times, 1994.

- *Strategy of protectionism*: U.S. steel companies seek 109% tax on foreign steel.
  The Boston Globe, 1994.

- *Strategy of financial restructuring*: Sears will sell its financial services company.
  The Wall Street Journal, 1994.

- *Strategy of brand names:* Timex has 50% of its domestic share of watches fall to 20% in one year.
  The Wall Street Journal Europe, 1993.

Executive Summary

The forces of change are sweeping through today's business environment, and yet our traditional responses are ineffective and doomed to failure. The sections that follow discuss each of these apparent prescriptions for success that are actually prescriptions for failure.

Solutions That Do Not Work

Since the 1980s, growth in productivity in many parts of the world dropped from +5% per year to under +1% (Europe, -1%, Japan -1%, USA +1%) per year. To correct this situation and to create long-term barriers to entry for competitors, some organizations took one or more of the following strategies:

- Cut costs

- Seek protectionist legislation

- Execute financial restructuring

- Promote brand names

These responses no longer provide a long-term barrier to entry and at best, with few exceptions, provide only short-term, competitive relief.

Cut Costs

The basic proposition is simple: If competitors produce my product or service more cheaply than I, then I ought to be able to do it, too. All that is required is the proper combination of wage, benefit, and personnel reductions, concessions from suppliers, increased production efficiencies . . . You know the equation. Find the right mix and prosperity will return.

The flaw in this strategy is that the main focus is often on reducing labor costs. Firing people does not create a long-term barrier to entry. Your competitors can do the same thing—you fire a person, they fire a person. Furthermore, this strategy (since it often focuses on laying off people) has a dampening effect on the surrounding region's economic vitality.

The exceptions are:

- Developing a short-term survival strategy in order to develop a long-term strategy

- Cutting costs to improve productivity, e.g., Return on Assests (ROA) increases as inventory levels drop

- Continuously cutting costs by moving down the learning curve, thus keeping ahead of your competition

The basic flaw of most cost-cutting strategies is that they are static and therefore easily copied by your competition. A dynamic strategy is needed.

Seek Protection

Unable to maintain high profits by competing on the basis of price, quality, or service, many organizations resort to clamoring for government protection from "unfair" competition. Never mind that "unfairness" depends entirely upon the perspective of the plaintiff. All that matters is that *my* organization will prosper (supposedly) behind the artificial walls of tariffs, quotas, and "voluntary" trade restrictions.

The problem with protectionism is that it functions as a sword with the same effectiveness and power that it does as a shield. Goods and services barred from competing in domestic markets find ready buyers *everywhere else*, where domestic products cannot compete favorably because of their relatively high prices. Behind the protective walls, shielded products vie for position in a sagging domestic market, which is forced to pay higher prices for products than if competition were unrestrained. And protectionism often produces retaliation.

Protectionism also produces a false sense of security in organizations by artificially suppressing competitive pressure. Such complacency leads to stagnation and atrophy in product development and innovation. When the protectionist period weakens or ends (as it inevitably does), the protected company is ill-equipped to meet the demands of the liberated marketplace. No one's interests (other than those profiting from artificially induced short-term gains) have been served.

Again, there are a few exceptions, such as fledgling industries or short-term help while a particular company gets back on its feet (e.g., Harley Davidson and Chrysler Corporation).

Execute Financial Restructuring

If organizations cannot make a profit selling products, perhaps there is money to be made buying and selling pieces of themselves. Such was the thinking during much of the 1970s, 1980s, and 1990s in boardrooms throughout the world, as corporate executives sought to generate revenues (as well as considerable personal wealth) through mergers, acquisitions, leveraged buyouts, and a host of other financial transactions largely unrelated to the core business of their corporations.

For example, Pan Am sold off its profitable routes in order to finance its unprofitable routes until it went out of business.

Organizations producing products are not necessarily good financial assets managers. Such financial restructuring produces no new jobs, inspires no product innovation, creates no efficiencies of production, and in no way alters the basic, underlying industrial and service engines that power a nation's economy and enrich its citizens' lives. Financial restructuring is ultimately only an idle distraction from the real job of providing useful products that meet the customers' needs.

Again, there are a few exceptions, such as when an entire industry (e.g., U.S. banking or hospitals) is consolidating or if technology is bringing industries together, as is the case with telecommunications and cable television.

Promote Brand Names

One classic strategy for maintaining and increasing market share is to establish finely tuned brand identities to which customers develop an allegiance. The global marketplace abounds with examples of successful branding efforts: Coca-Cola, Sony Walkman, Timex, Marlboro, Mercedes Benz, Stolichnaya vodka, brand name drugs, to name a few.

The trouble with this strategy is that consumers these days are a fickle lot. They may be able to name your product in a brand identification test, but they tend to purchase whatever is on sale this week—or, more importantly, whatever offers the highest value. Improvements in global communication and distribution systems, coupled with dramatic miniaturization of many product components, put everyone's goods and services into consumers' hands far more easily than in previous decades. And counterfeits or knockoffs, albeit illegal, are notoriously easy to produce and distribute, and notoriously difficult and expensive to combat.

You can no longer count on brand identity to ensure your product's success in the marketplace.

This was dramatically demonstrated when in 1993 Marlboro announced that it would reduce the price of its cigarettes to compete with the generic brands. That day, the "brand name" companies lost $50 billion in market capitalization on the New York Stock Exchange!

The exception is this: Promoting brand names as a strategy works only if it is coupled with the strategy of continuously adding value.

Conclusion—Seek a New Strategy

Despite the best efforts, the traditional "common sense" business solutions to the challenges of today's business environment are ill-suited to the task. All these strategies are static.

What is needed is a dynamic strategy—one that your competition cannot simply mimic instantly, but rather one that creates a dynamic barrier to entry based on a continuing series of improvements. The key is to develop an IT strategy that is as speedy as your business strategy itself.

Successful leaders need a new strategy: one that empowers their organizations to meet the needs of their customers in a way that creates a strategic business advantage over their competitors. The strategy must also provide an infrastructure that continuously accommodates change. The next chapter lays the foundation for just such a strategy. But as a preview, the successful strategy continuously adds value to your products and services.

Note that *speed* is the key. It ensures the following:

- Faster to market
- Continuously higher product quality — faster than your competitors
- Continuously lower cost — fast
- Continuous product improvement — fast
- Continuously adjusting pricing strategies
- Continuous adaptation to other sources of supply
- Continuously moving and broadening markets
- Etc.

All of these must be supported by a *fast, continuously* adaptable IT infrastructure.

3

The Correct Business Strategy: From High Volume to High Value

"In the high-value enterprise, profits derive not from scale and volume but from continuous discovery of new linkages between solutions and needs."

> Robert B. Reich,
> U.S. Secretary of Labor
> *The Work of Nations*

"We need to add value to our product to differentiate it from the competition."

> Jack Leckie, Vice President
> ALCOA

"The only way to improve competitive edge is through value enhancement."

> S.M. Datta, Chairman
> Hindustan Lever Limited
> Bombay, India

"Our business goal is to create a permanent competitive advantage."

> Jim Baroffro, President
> Chevron Canada Resources

"Our main business issues are speed of action/reaction/innovation, supply chain management, and customer service management."

Umberto Romdani, Chairman
Sagit—Italy

The Correct Solution: Dynamically Adding Value

In the past, changes in the business environment were paced at longer intervals, which allowed "static," one-time actions to become a barrier to entry. For example, a major barrier to entry would be massive volume. No longer! General Motors accounted for 3% of the GNP of the U.S. in 1980. No one could seriously top their high volume production. But by 1990, computer-aided design and transportation advances made it possible to manufacture anywhere in the world and assemble any units of volume at a continuously lowering cost. In 1994, Mercedes Benz will manufacture in India and Alabama! Tomorrow, where?

The correct business strategy—that products and services must be continuously improved and upgraded— is valid for the years to follow. The difference today is that products and services can be continuously improved with technological enhancement. Crucial areas include:

- Continuous improvement in the quality of products
- Ease of doing business
- Faster time to market
- Continuous cost reduction

- Higher overall quality

- Better customer service

- Customer focus

The implementation of each of these added value areas often involves numerous databases inside and outside the organization.

Executive Summary

Rather than pursuing the failed strategies of the past, successful businesses of the next decade must be committed *to adding value continuously to their products and services.* Information technology plays a pivotal role in an organization's ability to add value. You must create a new, strategic information infrastructure, because traditional information technology is too cumbersome, too slow, and too costly. You must establish a solid IT architecture for all business applications in order to create strategic advantage and to position your organization for breakthrough results. That new architecture is 3-tiered, client server, and standards-based.

Traditions within IT are Inadequate

Thus far, we have seen that organizations everywhere face major challenges to their success, and that the traditional IT mechanisms for coping with such challenges are no longer adequate. The following are additional examples of organizations held hostage by their antiquated information architectures:

- A hospital faces the threat of losing its accreditation because of its inability to reconcile its billing and patient care files.

- A major jet engine parts manufacturer faces a possible shutdown if it cannot comply with Federal Aviation Administration demands for tracking parts from assembly room floor to final customer.

- A major airline faces indictment for an inaccurate maintenance system.

- A major securities firm and a bank merge, but are unable to seize the strategic opportunity of presenting a single, unified customer interface due to incompatible computer systems.

- An insurance company is losing business due to its 15-day lag in processing automobile insurance applications.

- A large city government faces an ongoing revenue crisis due in part to millions of dollars in delinquent payments for municipal services.

New Information Technology Is the Key

While facing very different challenges, these organizations have one common characteristic: They are facing problems whose solutions lie in the use of *strategic information technology*, but they have been hampered by traditional IT.

When is an information system strategic? *It is strategic when it enables an organization to meet its highest goals, giving that organization a competitive advantage, be it basic survival, higher profit, or increased revenues.*

Few organizations can afford to ignore strategic information technology. Those that do will find competitors using strategic information technology to tighten the screws on them. An organization's competitive lead, gained through the first strategic application in an industry, has historically proven to be very difficult and costly, if not impossible, to displace (e.g., American Airlines' SABER system, Microsoft's DOS, Walmart's supply chain automation, Unilever's ice cream box).

Traditional IT Is Too Cumbersome

If an application is strategic, you need it *now,* and it will continuously change. However, even the most innovative and determined senior managers face a formidable barrier: Traditional information technologies are not geared toward the rapid production and change of information systems, strategic or otherwise.

We designed traditional IT technologies to support the back office (e.g., billing, accounting, payroll) and business strategies of the last two decades. As we discussed, these business strategies were static and could withstand long development cycles. It is not the fault of Management Information Systems departments (MIS) that it has the wrong technologies and infrastructures. It was correct for *then.* It is not for *now!*

(Appendix B, *Architectures that Do Not Work*, discusses the technical limitations of traditional approaches in more detail.)

Can you just buy your strategic application? No, because if the application is strategic, it is not "off the shelf." Also, buying something off the shelf does not create a barrier to entry. Off the shelf applications may be important but they are not strategic. For strategic applications, the implementation probably entails re-engineering the business, building bridges between internal devices and departments, and bringing external organizations into closer contact with the system.

From an information architecture point of view, the solution involves taking different types of information from inside and outside the organization, processing it, and presenting it in a form that is readily accessible to the right people. Such a solution is possible using a *client-server architecture,* since it allows your IT components to be used as "Lego" sets.

Traditional IT Is Too Slow and Too Costly

How long will it take to implement a new process or idea, and how much will it cost? Typical estimates for developing a major application are three to four years and millions of dollars. Despite such investments, finished applications often deliver far less than the originally envisioned capabilities—if they are completed at all.

For example, Boeing has been attempting to develop a common Bill of Materials for eight years. It takes Boeing, like many corporations, an average of 250 days to implement a change to its mainframe applications.

Such "runaway" systems—systems that run over budget and behind schedule—are increasingly becoming the rule rather than the exception. And they often end up costing much more than money.

"Blue Cross/Blue Shield United of Wisconsin attempted to maintain its customer base against inroads by popular HMOs by developing a $200 million computer system. As a result of fatal system flaws, the company lost 35,000 of its policy holders, distributed $60 million in overpayments and duplicate checks, and crippled customer services before the system could be brought under control."

The Boston Globe, 1992.

Even when an organization is the first to introduce a strategic application, a delay of several years for development and testing means that the new system is outdated by the time it is installed. The business goals and operating environment of an organization keep changing. *Strategic opportunities are moving targets.* The strategic opportunities of today will likely be irrelevant two years from now.

MIS departments are not to blame for the time lag. These organizations are limited by the technologies and methodologies with which they are equipped. Therefore, it's the technology and inadequate methodologies that are to blame.

Frustratingly enough, another important element of strategic applications—the data—usually resides on various computers inside and outside the organization. If these systems could only be linked, the strategic applications would emerge readily. Unfortunately, the information architectures of most organizations are not flexible and robust enough to integrate different computer systems smoothly, if at all.

Yet the business functions are integrated. For example, the inputs of an organization's capital, labor, energy, and materials are organized around the functions of a company (e.g., manufacturing, marketing, shipping, service, etc.), whereas the strategic opportunities are often cross-functional. For example, processes to improve quality, time to market, etc., all cut across many functions.

IT's challenge is to harmonize with the speed of business and the cross-functionality of business opportunities.

The Gap Between Business and IT Must Be Closed

Strategic Applications

As we noted, the root of the problem is not the MIS department or the people in the department. The fundamental problem is that business strategies keep changing (at a rate faster than ever before), and traditional IT cannot adapt that quickly. IT has traditionally supported the tactical, static, back-room functions, and its technologies have been suited for that purpose.

To close this gap, organizations must recognize that they need to approach strategic information applications in a way far removed from traditional application development. Organizations must adopt four special weapons:

- These crucial, high-payoff systems require quick *implementation technologies* and *special methodologies*.

- A *partnership* with IT personnel, users, strategic planners, and non-technical managers must drive the application building process, ensuring that they will use the system and that end results will meet strategic needs.

- These applications are continuously changing, and so must be supplied by an *architecture* that is dynamic, flexible, and cuts across functions.

- These applications must be supported by a *business case* that can withstand close scrutiny regarding economic justification; potential applications should be prioritized by their expected business payoffs.

Only recently have such special weapons and tactics begun to emerge, and only this year do we have the technologies to support them. A growing number of organizations have turned to the new approach advocated in this book. They have built strategic applications in two months, rather than two to five years. These applications have had more impact on their organizations than conventional applications because they were designed and built in a twelfth to a thirteenth of the time, and by business managers rather than by technicians. And most important, the applications were built on a new infrastructure—an architecture that can adapt continuously to change in business and technology.

<u>Tactical Applications - Your Existing IT</u>

Advancements made in hardware technology, especially in the speed and cost reduction of microprocessors, led to new opportunities for you. The existing mainframes—so called "legacy systems"— can serve as repositories of data, or servers, in the new infrastructure.

The opportunity exists to port your applications from mainframes to less expensive platforms. You have heard the buzz words: "downsize," "rightsize," "correctsize." When should this be done? Chapter 5 will tell you and detail the options you have with respect to your existing systems.

And this is not an untested approach. Corporations with high technology products, including Wall Street organizations, communications giants, manufacturers, retailers, and government agencies have already begun the move away from traditional IT. They are now doing so with the formal architecture explained in this book, and they have pioneered this approach with open systems tools and products. They have found that it not only works, but it also presents new business opportunities.

If you do not begin to think strategically about information technology—if you allow the ghost of the proprietary, structured, centralized thinking of the past to haunt your decision making—be guaranteed that you will eventually have a mess of cheap, unconnected applications that are not in harmony with your business.

A Client-Server Architecture Is Required

The only solution that empowers your business to realize fully the strategic advantages you need is a 3-tiered client-server architecture based on industry-standard open systems. Let's examine a high-level description of the concept and see how it has revolutionized the businesses that have implemented it.

The Simplicity of the Client-Server Architecture

Client-server, 3-tiered architecture involves separating the following application functions into three tiers:

- *Presentation* (or user interface), a tier that supports human-computer interaction using devices like the keyboard, mouse, and monitor.

- *Functionality*, connectivity, and database servers, which run on one or more computers to:
  - Connect to your existing systems
  - Connect to new databases
  - Connect to on-line services
  - Accept real-time feeds of data
  - Run and display applications across networks and sites
  - Process and formulate data
  - Interact with the desired user interfaces
  - Maintain security, audit trails, version control, and other system functions

- *Data* that may include existing systems and applications, and new databases that have been encapsulated to take advantage of this architecture with a minimum of transitional programming effort.

When users interact with a new strategic application built on this architecture, they deal only with the presentation layer; the servers interact with the databases or existing legacy systems to manipulate the information that the user requires.

All software in this architecture is characterized as either a client (software that makes requests) or a server (software that grants requests).

Communication between clients and servers must follow Distributed Computing Environment (DCE) standards as set by the Open Systems Foundation (OSF). These standards are implemented by every major vendor and can be used in conjunction with application tools developed by Open Environment Corporation (OEC). Note that the three tiers are *not* hardware tiers. All three can exist on the same machine or on many.

The servers can exist on *any vendor's* computer hardware, provided it has DCE-compliant connectivity, network management, and interface tools.

3-Tiered Client-Server Architecture

PRESENTATION	FUNCTIONALITY	DATA

User Interface — Functionality & Connectivity

Legacy Systems

New Data

NetMinder
Naming Server | Security Server — Machine A
Functionality Server — Machine B
Asynchronous Connectivity Server
SQL Database Server — Machine C

The Benefits of Client-Server Architecture

Some software and hardware vendors (such as Powersoft, Oracle Card, and Oracle) promote a 2-tiered architecture that has the presentation and functionality tiers tied together. Such architecture will cripple your organization—do not use it unless you break the two ti-ers into three!

The 2-tiered architecture will lock you into a proprietary software that is not industrial strength for scalable applications.

By separating an application into three tiers (presentation, functionality servers, and data), your organization gains the following:

- Freedom to select any database management system

- Dynamic backup

- Freedom to select any graphical user interface

- Flexibility to add new technologies as needed

- On-line access to any data sources

- Lower cost of hardware

- Freedom to select the hardware of the appropriate size

- Openness for continuous added value

- Support for a migration strategy from old systems

- Preservation of your current hardware and software investment

- Parallel development of applications

- Different user views of data

- Security

- High transaction, two-phase commit

- Robustness and fault tolerance

Again, note that 3-tiered does *not* mean 3 hardware boxes. The software can be placed on one box or distributed in as many as you want.

The Client-Server Architecture Gets Results

This is more than theory. The 3-tiered client-server architecture produces tangible results. Here are two case studies describing systems that were implemented using Open Environment Corporation (OEC) tools.

National Tax Board of Sweden

The National Tax Board of Sweden controls data, operations, and offices for the government of Sweden's tax system. The policies of this board affect every citizen.

The business opportunity: To improve time and resource allocation in order to provide better service to Swedish taxpayers.

The technological obstacle: The National Tax Board operates many independent offices throughout the country. Levels of service and priorities vary greatly from office to office. A task that may consume 50% of the resources of one office may be inconsequential to another office.

If an individual office wants to improve efficiency by using superior methods that differ from those used in other offices, the office chief must call the central IT department in Stockholm or other independent offices and make a request. Even an ambitious office chief could encounter difficulties because it is often unclear what data is needed or who should be contacted for the information.

Instead of fixing the same procedures in separate offices repeatedly, the Tax Board wanted to improve communications among offices. This would allow them to compare procedures, improve effectiveness, and share solutions to common problems.

The solution using OEC tools: The Tax Board built a user-friendly application that allows office chiefs to access resource and time sheet information in real time, and to enhance communications between offices throughout the country. With this application, office chiefs are able to compare resource allocation and the amount of time that workers spend on various tasks. This allows offices to have the same set of priorities and allocate resources properly. The central office in Stockholm can measure overall productivity by utilizing previously inaccessible data.

The business benefit: The new system allows offices to take advantage of better resource allocation in other offices and sends a consistent message to citizens and other tax offices.

United HealthCare

United HealthCare (UHC) is a health care management corporation composed of 27 health plans and specialty care management organizations. UHC serves purchasers, users, managers, and providers of health care.

The business opportunity: To process claims more efficiently.

The technological obstacle: UHC's batch processing system was not synchronized with Claims Administration. The claims service was administered by batch reports printed and mailed to UHC organizations once a week. Any information critical to the resolution of a claim that was added after the weekly printing was unknown to the claims administrators until the following week. Sometimes, claims were lost or sent to the wrong administrator. In other situations, some claims were not printed and so were never processed. This problem was made worse by the additional time that it took to discover the missing claims.

The architecture of UHC's mainframe computer made modifying applications difficult.

The solution using OEC tools: Using OEC tools, UHC built a graphical user interface as a front-end server to make calculations and access the databases containing all claims information.

The business benefit: The new standards-based system eliminates 95% of the claims rework effort (thus enhancing productivity) and ensures that customers receive payments faster (thus improving customer satisfaction).

Freeing the MIS Hostages

In addition to the two organizations whose cases are highlighted above, the organizations whose problems were listed earlier in this chapter used the new client-server approach to develop strategic applications to help conquer their respective challenges. Here is a brief description of each of their solutions.

- **The Hospital**
  Goal: Retain accreditation by reconciling billing and patient-tracking capabilities.
  Solution: An information system that immediately provides a patient's medical history, current diagnosis, room number, attending physicians, treatment, and insurance status, with a running total of the bill.

- **The Engine Parts Manufacturer**
  Goal: Track each part from the factory to the final user by serial number.

Solution: An information system that allows engineers to enter part and serial numbers and displays a graphical picture of the entire engine. Engineers can "page" down to the desired part by pointing, and can maintain single-point tracking of each part's life cycle.

- **The Airline**
  Goal: Automate the maintenance system.
  Solution: A global information system that integrates the maintenance and engineering systems and meets Federal Aviation Administration standards.

- **The Securities Firm**
  Goal: Provide complete financial service to customers.
  Solution: An information system that seamlessly integrates the organizations' systems to provide company personnel and customers with a single interface for both banking and investment services.

- **The Automobile Insurance Company**
  Goal: Retain share of auto insurance business by decreasing the time it takes to approve an application.
  Solution: An information system that automatically retrieves driver data from state motor vehicle databases and compares the data to information from company databases, reducing the approval cycle from fifteen days to one day.

- **The City Government**
  Goal: Improve collection rates on delinquent payments.

Solution: An information system that consolidates billing for property taxes, water, municipal court fees, and police charges.

In addition to these organization's major strategic applications that are being rolled out in 1994, add Freddie Mac, ALCOA, United Technology, Woolworth, Unilever, W. Granger, General Electric, the state of Michigan, the state of Utah, etc.

Conclusion

Information technology based on a 3-tiered client-server architecture and open systems represents the key that can unlock the vast potential for harmonizing your IT with your business strategy. Best of all, that potential can be realized in an amazingly short time, because the client-server approach brings implementation speed as well as flexibility. Next, we will lay out a straightforward process for exploiting this new technology within your organization *today*. All that you need to supply is the determination to make it happen.

First Steps

1. Examine the challenges currently facing your organization. Identify those that you think may be addressed using information technology. (We will see how to decide which challenges to tackle. For now, just identify them.)

2. Resolve to lead your organization forward in a commitment to the 3-tiered client-server architecture.

3. Contact systems vendors to receive training and tools that support a 3-tiered client-server architecture based on open systems and DCE-compliant tools.

4

A Method for Re-engineering Your Business Processes

"Information concerns: To identify major strategic applications to enhance each operation's competitive position."

Andre De Botton, CEO
Mesbla SA (Brazil)

"'Solutions' to strategic problems are not found by detached analysts focusing coolly on the problem."

Graham Allison, Harvard University,
Essence of Decision.

"I accept the challenge . . . to initiate a change in the way we think, to be able to identify and implement the strategic applications that really will fulfill our motto of, 'We Can Make A Difference!'"

Mary Solmonson, Director
Continental Airlines

Executive Summary

To find the appropriate strategic applications, use the following method:

- Assemble a group of business executives, users, and IT personnel.

- Agree on the organization's goals.

- Agree on the organization's "critical success factors" (CSFs), which are mechanisms for achieving the goals.

- Identify the key processes involved in those critical success factors.

- For each of those processes, articulate the way that they are presently accomplished.

- Re-engineer the process to improve its effectiveness (radically, if you have top management support; otherwise, incrementally).

- Identify where IT can help in the re-engineered process.

- Identify the external competitive forces that confront your organization.

- For each of the forces, develop a business strategy, e.g., use IT to match their goals, buy them, out-price them, etc.

- Identify hidden treasures—other benefits of the information.

- Build a business care for justification, discipline, and monitoring.

- Continuously repeat this process.

Professor Michael Porter of Harvard, Mr. Michael Hammer, my former teaching assistant at MIT, and others have written about numerous examples of strategic applications resulting from re-engineering organizations. Their examples, as well as all of the cases in this book, could be identified using the method above.

Let us just elaborate on two of the steps. Together, all of these steps form the strategic model. You must not "outsource" any of these steps. In fact, you must keep in-house control of all steps for strategic applications. While you may have partners help you, you must use this process to maximize your barriers to entry.

CEO Frustration

According to Paul Strassmann, author of *The Business Value of Computers*, recent surveys of some 200 Fortune 500 corporations reveal:

- 52% of these organizations spent more money on IT than they made in profits. The CEOs rightly ask, "What did I get?"

- When organizations are grouped by industry (e.g., insurance, banking) and then ranked by profit, the answer to the question, "Do the best spend more money on IT?" is a resounding "No!". Everyone in the industry spent the same number of IT dollars per employee. It is not *how much* you spend on IT, but *where* you spend it that counts.

- The best companies spent 80% of their IT budget on operational systems (sales, services, etc.) and

20% on back office systems. The worst spent just the opposite: 80% of their IT budget on back office systems!

The moral: *Spend your IT money on strategic applications.*

Making a Business Case

There are three reasons why a business case is a necessary step in building a strategic system. First, it provides a valuable cost justification. Second, the completed analysis disciplines the users and technical people by setting budgetary goals. Finally, the projected benefits can only be realized by monitoring the system during operation. The business case establishes a necessary baseline for such measurement.

Justification

Below is a list of savings or revenue producing opportunities that we at CTGroup have seen organizations experience from using client-server systems:

- Increased revenues per sales call
- Increased revenues per telephone minute
- Increased revenue by cross sell
- Increased revenue from unrelated services
- Recaptured market share
- Increased customer satisfaction
- Reduced training costs
- Reduced errors
- Reduced data redundancy
- Decreased inventory costs
- Eliminated overtime

- Reduced hardware costs
- Reduced administrative costs
- Redirected employees' time
- Reduced waste of resources
- Reallocated "freed working capital"
- Closed fixed assets no longer needed
- Decreased operating costs

Critical success factors help you determine if an application is truly strategic. But is that enough to justify undertaking the project? Many managers feel that it is, especially those who make decisions based on a qualitative, intuitive grasp of a situation.

For most managers, the litmus test of a strategic application is a cost-benefit worksheet that answers the key question: "What is the payoff?"

Discipline

Applications based on a 3-tiered client-server architecture and ODE tools are easy to change, both in response to changes in technology and to users' requests for additional features. Consequently, it is critical that you prioritize business and IT activities to ensure that they stay focused on the most critical issues. How can you maintain this focus? The business case, coupled with a functionality matrix, is the answer.

The Functionality Matrix

As a framework for prioritizing proposed system functionality, we find it helpful to have users and technical personnel construct a matrix. The rows list the critical processes of your business and each column lists the features associated with those processes.

The management team then estimates the benefit, cost, and "emotional-desire" values for each of the features. When the estimates are complete, select the 20% of the features that yield 80% of the desired benefits. Implement this set first. With the 3-tiered client-server architecture you can continue to add the remaining features while the system is being productively used. Your case has been made! And an implementation plan will focus on those 20%.

The following example illustrates a matrix for the order-entry system of a major telephone company. Business functions for the company include making sales, taking customer orders, and answering questions about configuration options for telephones and other products and services. A variety of features characterize each function. For example, the company can take orders through telemarketing calls, in writing in response to direct mail campaigns, through calls to Customer Service, etc. The company can specify product configurations for its own products (phone color, style, feature set, etc.), and potentially for other products and services as well (cable television, utilities, community services, etc.).

For each cell in the matrix, a cost and benefit number is determined. Often an "emotional desirability" weight is also established for each cell. The cells in each row are then ordered by the highest benefit and emotional desirability.

Functions	Features			
Selling	Customer Service	Cross sell		
Taking Orders	Telemarketing activities	Direct mail	Customer Service	
Configuration	Phone products	Other products	Price info.	Financing programs

With the matrix completed, the company can determine which features are the most critical (using the 20%-for-80% rule mentioned above) and thus most worthy of being addressed.

Monitoring

To ensure that the organization implements the business changes needed to achieve the benefits described earlier in the "Justification" section, you must monitor the financial benefits of the program.

Often traditional measures such as ROI, ROA, or ROA (Profit/Assets) will suffice. For example, ALCOA has two billion in inventory. A system to reduce this would be strategic, and its effectiveness could be monitored by ROA. However, you will have to be creative to define a measurement for monitoring the success of many applications. Let's just mention two areas.

If you are implementing a decision support system, a measure like Return on Management (ROM = Profit/Management Expense) may be appropriate. If the decisions are better, then profit should increase; if the new system is effective, then management expense should decrease.

For the public sector or the not-for-profit sector, develop measures such as Return on Budget (e.g., ROB =

Number of Cases Processed/Budget), where the numerator is your objective.

Building and Deploying the Application

Once you have identified your strategic application (based on the CSFs that support your organization's goals) and established the necessary business case, it is time to build and deploy it. While these are certainly not trivial tasks, CTGroup's methodology using ODE tools allows you to field an industrial-strength system *in no more than 20 weeks.* Given the proper infrastructure and staffing, this process consists of a "pilot" system phase lasting one to three weeks, followed by a "production" system phase lasting 10 to 20 weeks. Compare this development time to the one to six *years* that traditional systems require for development and testing.

Hidden Treasures

Before we conclude this chapter, we must stress one final point. Fortunately, this last point is very good news.

Implementing applications in the client-server architecture using ODE tools in your organization will lead to the discovery of "hidden treasures:" profitable business opportunities that emerge unexpectedly from the firm foundation of your new information systems.

After successfully applying the strategic model and arriving at a winning application idea, it is sensible to go back through the model to discover ways of reaping more benefits. Are there other CSFs that the system might be able to address? Are there different goals whose CSFs can be supported through the same application?

Blue Cross/Blue Shield wanted an application that would help protect market share from encroaching on health maintenance organizations. An associated critical success factor was to improve its ability to respond to customer inquiries about claims. The company designed an application to be installed on computer terminals in public places, allowing customers to receive information about policies and claims in the same way they would use a bank's automated teller machines.

The Blue Cross executives reexamined the strategic model and considered a second organizational goal: entering new insurance markets. One critical success factor for this goal was making it easy for customers to find out about and purchase Blue Cross's new life insurance products. The executives realized that the same application could be extended to support this new CSF. The public terminals could encourage customers to retrieve information on life insurance prices and benefits, and Blue Cross could sell the insurance immediately!

There is even more mileage to be squeezed out of the model. *By turning the process around, the application can lead to new business strategies—and new lines of business.*

Many organizations find they are able to devise unique strategies based on their applications. Such unexpected opportunities can be the most exciting aspect of planning and deploying a strategic application.

Royal Caribbean Cruise Lines (RCCL) built a strategic application with a facsimile machine network to connect travel agents to their booking office for faster confirmations and increased bookings. After utilizing this tool successfully, RCCL realized that they had also created an excellent new advertising vehicle.

The American Automobile Association (AAA) created a strategic application that unified client membership and service call information. Once the system was up and running, AAA realized that automotive product retailers (such as stores eager to sell replacement batteries to people phoning AAA for a jump-start) would pay handsomely for access to service call information—so handsomely, in fact, that AAA could offer free memberships to customers willing to release this information!

Some managers may question whether their organizations are likely to achieve similar unexpected rewards from a strategic application. *We have found that such payoffs are more the rule than the exception. Most organizations face a limitless number of business opportunities; taking advantage of these opportunities requires only imagination and the proper tools.* The strategic model can help point the way.

Conclusion

By deciding to control your strategic applications with in-house resources, highlighting those applications that really are strategic, building a valid business case, and exploiting hidden treasures, you will have done all that is necessary to position your company for a new era of IT empowerment. More important, you will have ensured that strategic applications will be ready and waiting to generate significant competitive advantage in the marketplace.

First Steps

1. Separate and identify the goals and CSFs of your organization with your colleagues. These

are not set in stone. An organization's goals and CSFs should be reevaluated and modified over time. Examine the processes that support the CSFs. Re-engineer the processes. Identify the *IT applications* to support these re-engineered processes.

2. Identify the external forces affecting your organization's competitive position (e.g., customers, legislators, suppliers).

3. Identify the goals and CSFs of these external forces.

4. Identify ways in which your organization can aid these organizations in attaining their goals by using information technology, thus turning these forces into allies. Identify *IT applications* that reduce these competitive threats.

5. Seek out your present *strategic opportunities*. Be willing to dream. Rank these ideas in order of their benefit to you and to your organization.

6. Identify an individual or several individuals who can dedicate themselves to making your vision a reality. Provide them with the proper training and tools to execute your opportunity. The individuals you select should be given the support they require, but should feel *the urgency* of your opportunity.

7. Begin to construct a business case and functionality matrix for the application you have identified.

8. Involve the users of the system! Form a committee of users whose mission is to provide

you with *their* ideas on savings and revenue. Who knows better than the users how much time is saved or how much more effective they can be with client-server architecture?

9. Estimate the development cost of the application using both traditional methods and client-server architecture. As a rule of thumb, we have found that cost is reduced by 40% to 80% using client-server architecture and ODE tools.

10. Analyze the business estimate and determine which figures are crucial to the final total. Quantify! Quantify! Quantify!

11. Commit to using the 3-tiered client-server architecture. It's your only choice.

5

IT Strategy—A Business Framework

"What are the costs of downsizing, migrating from mainframes, stovepipe systems?"

> Robert Sacks, Director
> Grumman

"We face a massive process of migration/downsizing."

> Col. Joe Guirreri, Commander
> Disa - Europe

"Concerned with the strategic alignment of the IT function with business."

> Bruce Handel, Director
> Indian and Northern Affairs, Canada

"Need to move from mainframe/midrange to client server."

> Bill McCloneo, CIO
> Westinghouse

"Concerned about the business transition from legacy mainframe environments."

Eugene Bailey, Senior Director
Information Systems
Motorola

Executive Summary

This chapter provides a framework for evaluating your IT options as you would evaluate a business.

The need to treat IT evaluation as a business was dramatically pointed out by Mr. James Duckworth, current CIO of Unilever and former CFO of the ice cream division of Unilever.

Unilever's ice cream division developed a creative business strategy: Give small ice cream retailers an ice cream box refrigerator on the condition they only stock Unilever's ice cream. They grew to over 40% of the market in Europe.

Mr. Duckworth said that he could calculate to the penny the benefits and costs of each ice cream box. Now, as the CIO of all of Unilever, he has not been able to calculate the benefits and cost of each of the computer "boxes"—a common problem and manifested by the common CEO perception of IT being a "cost."

Let us stop the view of IT as only a cost and approach IT as a business!

IT Strategy

The three tables on the following pages present a framework for evaluating the options in the following categories:

- Your existing systems
- New decision-support systems
- New transaction systems

The first table shows four options that you have with existing IT "boxes" and applications in your organization:

- *Re-Face.* Simply leave the existing applications on their existing machines (e.g., mainframes) and add a mechanism to access them from another machine. Typical mechanisms include "screen scraping," pier-to-pier, and gateways. Thus, you realize a business benefit from access and incur a small cost for implementing the access mechanism. However, there are no IT savings or maintenance savings, since you still have the same machines and applications.

- *Re-Host.* Port the applications from larger, expensive machines to less expensive machines with the same environment. This is sometimes called "downsizing" or "rightsizing." The application code is not changed. Thus, the hardware is usually less expensive.

- *Re-Architect.* Rewrite the application, separating it into three components: presentation, functionality, and database. In this way it is much easier

73

to maintain the software and thus obtain an IT maintenance savings. The business will benefit not only from access, but also from the speed of changes—a further increase-in-business benefit.

As the president of Miles, Inc., stated, "Everything in my business must be fast—speed to market, new product development, etc. The slowest thing is my IT development."

- *Re-Engineer.* Re-engineer the entire process captured by the IT applications. Rewrite the applications to reflect the new, re-engineered process, thus opening up the possibility of an enormous business benefit.

You must then calculate the cost of the infrastructure for this architecture: training, network, tools, data cleanup, etc.

For each application and each computer, the matrix in the following table can be used as a guide to the business analysis.

Existing Applications

IT Strategy Options	Business Benefits	IT Hardware Savings	IT Maintenance Savings	Costs: Hardware Personnel Software
Re-Face (Surround)	$ ¥	—	—	$ ¥
Re-Host (Port/transfer)	$ ¥	$ ¥	—	$$ ¥
Re-Architect (3-tiered/ replace)	$$ ¥¥	$ ¥	$ ¥	$$$ ¥¥¥
Re-Engineer (Process)	$$$$$ ¥¥¥¥¥	$ ¥	$ ¥	$$$$ ¥¥¥¥

The next table describes the two options you have for Decision Support Systems (DSS). The first allows you to use an architecture in which all the data exists in a "legacy system." In the second, you must create new databases. Both options use the 3-tiered client-server architecture.

New Decision Support

IT Stragegy Options	Business Benefits	Architecture
For some data, leave existing system (e.g., 3-tiered)	ROA ROE ROM	
Build all-new database (3-tiered)		

The last table presents a framework for analysis and the options for transaction systems. The difference between DSS and transaction systems is that a transaction monitor (TM) is placed in the middle tier of the three tiers.

New Transaction System

IT Strategy Options	Architecture
For some data, leave existing system 3-tiered using transaction processing, CICS, ENCINA . . .	
Build all-new database (3-tiered) using transaction processing, CICS, Kerberos security, ENCINA . . .	

Conclusion

IT can be treated as a business.

First Step

Use the matrix provided as a framework to make your evaluations. Use Migration Strategies models or contact the various consultant and hardware firms that are using these models.

6

Client-Server Technology: Architecture of Empowerment that Will Work

"Each location has its own home grown systems which are unable to communicate with each other."

Richard A. Kocerha, President
ALCOA

"Information needs are very great at this time. Lack of timely, crisp information is our major limiting factor to improve profitability and growth—help."

Carmine F. Bosco
V.P. & General Manager
Ingersoll-Rand Company

"It's exciting to think that IT can actually support us rather than constrain us."

Marsha Shuler
Federal Reserve Bank of Richmond

"[The] biggest paradigm change for me was the degree to which open, client-server solutions can be done now, today! Much more feasible than I imagined."

Thomas A. Ford
Procter & Gamble

"The most significant benefit to me is the realization that 3-tiered computing is the most effective way to architect the open environment."

Tom Hoburn, Director
Hewlett Packard

Executive Summary

Client-server technology provides the foundation on which to build the strategic information applications that can energize and empower your business. The 3-tiered architecture—presentation, functionality, data—allows you to:

- Build applications rapidly
- Modify them easily as business circumstances dictate
- Connect to other systems
- Evolve to new architecture
- Involve users directly in design and development to ensure maximum usability and effectiveness

The 3-Tiered Client-Server Architecture

Client-server architecture provides all of the functionality required by today's strategic applications. *The old systems need not be altered.* The new system can be built quickly and inexpensively because it uses a generic, "prefabricated" construction that does not require rebuilding the older systems' databases of information—a time-consuming part of building a new application.

Rapid application development (RAD) tools are the most significant advancement in getting applications up and running quickly. RAD tools are much more than mere graphical user interface (GUI) builders, which allow programmers to build front ends to applications. They provide the entire spectrum of programming tools for organizations that need to integrate old databases—and they also provide the GUI tools for good measure.

In most cases, a strategic application based on client-server architecture can be designed, built, and installed in months rather than years.

The client-server architecture involves separating application functions into the following three interchangeable components, or "tiers:"

- *Presentation tier* (or user interface). This tier interfaces with the user and consists of hardware such as a PC or workstation.

- *Functionality tier.* This tier provides functionality, connectivity, and database servers. It provides the bridge between the first and third tiers.

- *Data tier.* This tier may include existing systems, applications, and data that has been encapsulated to take advantage of this architecture with a minimum of transitional programming effort.

Users interact only with the presentation tier. The presentation "clients" communicate with the intermediate servers. These servers handle interaction with the databases or existing "legacy systems" and manipulate the information the user requires.

An example makes this clearer. Suppose we build an application that provides access to patient information in a hospital: real-time respiratory data, and outpatient financial and personal information in a DB2 database on a mainframe; clinical laboratory data on a Digital VMS system; radiology information on a Unisys machine; and insurance information on an external CICS 3090 at the insurance company.

Furthermore, we want to be able to exploit each source of data (which exists on many brands of hardware scattered throughout the United States) using UNIX workstations, Macintosh computers at home, or our notebook PCs when we're on the road.

Impossible? It may seem so, but free-flowing, flexible information access is straight-forward in a 3-tiered architecture as shown in the following figure. Observe the three layers. You can run any vendor's platform at the presentation layer. Any legacy system fits the bill for the data layer and database system. And for functionality, any language can be used.

What is important in the illustration is the communication between the clients and server. That communication will comply with DCE, DME, and later CORBA standards.

Hospital System

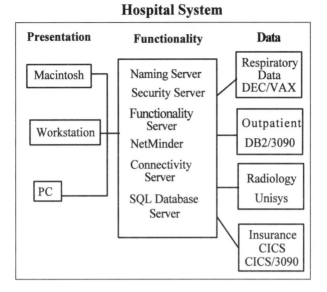

The Presentation Tier

The presentation tier provides the user interface that supports human-computer interaction through devices like the keyboard, mouse, voice recognition, monitor, personal computers, and workstations. The figure on the next page shows a partial list of software tools for constructing an interface on any of these devices.

**Presentation Tier
(Clients)**

Borland C/C++	Oracle Card
Camelot	Oracle SqlForms
Choreographer	PC-Interface
Contessa	PowerBuilder
Designer Workbench	Small Talk
Enfin	SuperCard
HyperCard	ToolBook
Jyacc	Uniface
Mozart	VermontViews
OpenLook	Visual Basic
Object Power	X/MOTIF

The Functionality Tier

The functionality tier is the heart of the application, where critical computing takes place. Servers and clients in this tier perform many functions:

- Authenticate users' identities to provide system security.

- Provide a consistent, user-transparent mechanism for naming files and directories across many different hardware and operating system protocols.

- Provide communication connections to external sources of data (such as CICS or DB2) and translate the data into the formats needed by the other server or clients.

- Provide special-purpose data manipulation functions, such as scanning the CICS data for material relevant to a user's query or synchronizing the updating of data across disparate databases.

- Provide transaction monitors (such as ENCINA, CICS, and TUXEDO) that perform backup recovery, audit trails, two-phase commits, and data integrity.

- Provide security for authenticity and validating security.

- Provide version control that keeps track of all software versions and manages updates.

- Provide the Broker, or naming server, which is a DCE function that keeps track of the location of all servers.

Adding another data connection to your application (such as importing information about corporate officers and facilities from a CD-ROM source) is as simple as plugging in one more servers that can communicate with the new data.

Note that for production systems, the servers in the functionality tier may reside on many different computers and, for robustness, may in fact be duplicated on different machines.

Also, in the 3-tiered architecture, any language can be used to implement the servers (e.g., C, C++, or OPS). The OEC tools described in Appendix B, *Traditional Architectures*, facilitate the construction of servers and provide NetMinder as the manager of this environment.

Functionality Tier (Servers)

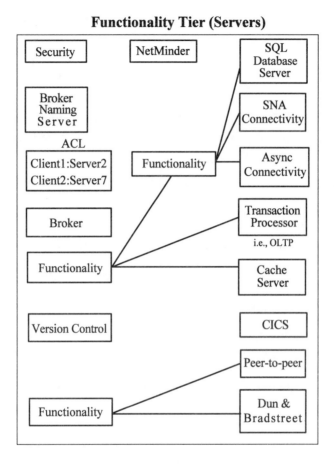

The Data Tier

The data tier consists of all the sources of information that your application ultimately seeks to reach and use. The user interface clients in the presentation tier only communicate with the data through the agency of the appropriate intermediate servers. Consequently, the types of data that may populate this tier are completely unrestrained. Any application may gain access to any type of data, on any system, in any location, provided that the appropriate server is in place. That's flexibility!

The following figure shows a partial list of the possible sources of data.

Data Tier

Oracle	Informix
Sybase DB/2 6000	CICS
Allbase	VMS
Flatfile	Dun & Bradstreet

The Versatility of Client-Server Architecture

There are several ways that moving your information technology infrastructure to the client-server model can benefit your organization. First, let's look at an example of how this new model benefited a small business, then discuss five of the most important gains for all types of organizations:

- Application development speed

- Migration to open systems and gradual downsizing

- System connectivity

- Evolution to a gateway architecture

- Applications built from scratch

Strategic Advantage for a Small Organization

Covenant Insurance wanted to reduce the time required to deliver auto insurance policy quotes to its agents. The information needed to process an application included:

- Premium and loss information stored on an IBM mainframe
- Policy quote and numbering information stored on a WANG computer
- Driver information kept on computers at the state's department of motor vehicles
- Financial business information from Dun and Bradstreet's computers

Covenant had been unable to tie together these 4 systems (two of which were owned by other organizations, and thus could not be altered). By using client-server architecture, however, Covenant built a system that retrieved the required information quickly from all four computers. A Covenant employee simply typed in the appropriate policy and driver's license numbers and the reports came back in seconds. The system was easy to use and allowed underwriters to make decisions instantly. The policy application-processing time was reduced from fifteen days to one day.

Rapid Development: Speed Is Everything

Some of the strategic applications achieved through client-server architecture could also be accomplished by traditional approaches; they would just take longer and cost more. *Time alone can make the difference between being in or out of business.*

Speed was crucial to a major hospital when it was notified by the State Board of Health that the hospital's difficulties in billing and documenting patient care might cost it its accreditation. The hospital's ability to build a patient information and billing system was absolutely critical to the organization's survival.

The hospital had all the information it needed in its existing data tier, and the users were familiar and comfortable with the equipment. *The hospital's problem was that it had no way of getting its computers to work together to provide effective billing and patient care systems.* Using client-server technology and building a strong functionality tier provided the required integration without duplicating the effort encapsulated in the existing system.

Rapid Development

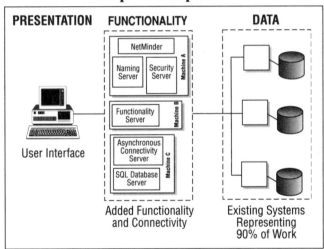

PRESENTATION **FUNCTIONALITY** **DATA**

NetMinder

Naming Server | Security Server

Machine A

Functionality Server

Machine B

Asynchronous Connectivity Server

SQL Database Server

Machine C

User Interface

Added Functionality and Connectivity

Existing Systems Representing 90% of Work

Migration to Open Systems

The client-server architecture can be a crucial bridge between the old and new environments, providing immediate and continuous access to the new strategic capabilities while the organization gradually replaces existing systems.

When a major international courier service decided to replace its multiple billing systems with a new, integrated worldwide billing system, it assumed that it would have to suffer with the old systems during the multi-year project development phase. Then the courier discovered that a client-server architecture could be brought up in just a few months. As the long-term version of the new system was built, it could be installed in pieces without interrupting the functioning of the old architecture. In addition, the courier had the option of replacing the old systems with an expanded version of client-server architecture or of building an entirely new environment.

Migration to Open Systems

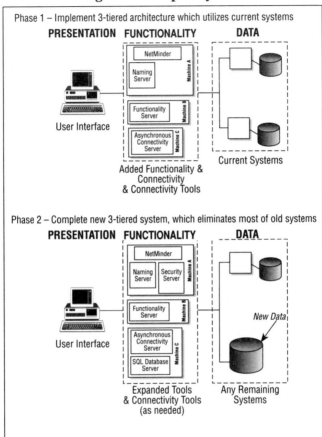

System Connectivity

Many organizations rely on personal computers to handle information applications. It's no wonder: PCs are inexpensive to operate and easy to use, and they provide individuals with greater control over their computer-dependent work. The problem with PCs is that PC applications are often of limited usefulness unless they have access to information that cannot be stored on the PC itself. *Some PC users need to plug into databases stored on giant corporate mainframe systems, for example, while others need access to databases kept outside the organization.*

Wellington Management encountered this problem. They needed to improve their portfolio management capability. Their information architecture did not allow connectivity between the customer's data in an HP timesharing system and real-time quotes. This prevented Wellington from determining risk positions on-line.

Using client-server architecture, Wellington Management's MIS staff was able to tie their PCs to the customer database and keep the database current with real-time quotes. This allowed instant updates and improved risk and portfolio management. The tie-in was "transparent" both to the users and to the remote system from which data was being retrieved and updated automatically from the PCs. Any other approach would have required scrapping the original system. This system was built in 8 weeks and is now installed on the desks of 200 financial managers.

System Connectivity on a Grander Scale

We have seen that client-server architecture is capable of obtaining and integrating information from one or two systems lying outside the organization. But some organizations formulate strategic application ideas that require tying into tens, or even hundreds, of outside computers representing a wide range of hardware and software environments. Difficult (at best) through conventional approaches, this process is straightforward using client-server architecture.

Consider the situation of one state's Department of Health, which wanted to collect patient information from nearly 300 independent hospitals scattered around the state. The team could have applied client-server architecture to the Health Department's IBM mainframe. But even this technology may have faltered given the task of incorporating 300 different interfaces into a single system. So the department tried another approach: Each outside system would receive its own small-scale client-server architecture to hide the incompatibilities of the different systems. The department's mainframe could then treat all 300 machines as if they were identical and compatible systems.

One problem remained: How could the hospitals be convinced to apply client-server architecture to their systems? Client-server architecture does not interfere with the normal functions of their systems, but MIS managers are typically wary of any alteration or addition to their environments. In addition, there was the cost of implementing the small-scale client-server architectures (about $30,000 per hospital), which the Health Department wanted each hospital to absorb. Providing the department with information was not much of an incentive for the hospitals to install the systems, so additional incentives had to be built into the system architecture. Fortunately, the client-server model makes such extensions easy to implement.

Every hospital in the U.S. must send information to a variety of public and private insurance institutions, as well as to research groups such as the National Cancer Registry. Since these varied reporting requirements bury hospitals in a costly mountain of paperwork, the Health Department rightly guessed that hospitals would welcome the chance to have patient information shipped automatically to each agency or institution via electronic mail or computer-printed letters in the format required by each organization.

Now the hospitals had something significant to gain: Client-server architecture linked the hospitals' registration, medical, and billing systems to improve patient care and cash flow, simultaneously sending the Health Department the information it needed. The system was introduced successfully throughout the state.

Evolution to a Gateway Architecture

One of the nation's top ten banks had no way of knowing, on any given day, how much money was in the bank, or where that money came from. A batch-oriented system compiled the bank's reports only once a month, making it impossible to determine how much money was in the bank at any given moment.

To solve this problem, the bank decided to move to an on-line system, with a huge data warehouse (a database machine such as those manufactured by Teradata) and on-line access. But the transition would take time —time that this bank did not have!

Client-server architecture solved the problem. The advent of high-powered, special-purpose database machines had made it possible to route data through a single machine dedicated solely to this purpose. With client-server architecture, this machine served as a "data gateway," allowing data to be moved between any application, system, or user interface.

Evolution to a Gateway Architecture

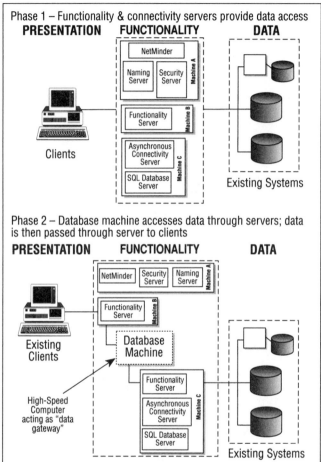

Phase 1 – Functionality & connectivity servers provide data access

Phase 2 – Database machine accesses data through servers; data is then passed through server to clients

Starting from Scratch: Building the Core Systems

A major U.S. organization needed to build a regional and national ordering and inventory system. The team built the 20 regional systems first, and then integrated them to produce the national system. After the core systems had been built using client-server architecture, adding specialized customer and management interfaces was straightforward.

Client-server architecture offers a modular, flexible, and easy approach to building new systems. The ability of this architecture to attach to many systems also applies when talking about subsystems within a single project. *Therefore, you can build your package in pieces and see each of those parts running, long before the final system is complete.*

Standards and Open Systems

Why is it important to define standards and open systems? For one thing, the growing confusion over open systems threatens to undermine the further development and acceptance of the concept.

Let us draw an analogy. Australia has seven states, each one with its own railroad system and each one with a different track gauge! Passengers have to disembark one train to get on another in order to cross their country. Does standardizing the color of the train help? No. Does standardizing the number of cars help? Of course not.

Only standardizing the gauge of the track will solve the problem. Similarly, there are many computer standards, as illustrated in the following table. The only standard that is *necessary*, however, is how clients communicate with servers. That standard is the Distributed Computing Environment (DCE) developed by Open Systems Foundation (OSF).

Standards Supporting 3-Tiered Architecture

Area	Standards	Bodies
Object Standards	CORBA DOMF SOM	CORBA
Distributed Client-Server Standards: RPC, Security, Naming	DCE ONC	OSF/DCE UI/ATLAS
Network Standards	TCP/IP IPX SLIP	OSI WINSOCK
Operating System Standards	UNIX OS/40 MPE MVS VMS OS/2 Windows	POSIX X/OPEN XPG

So what is an open system? Some will say that an open system is software, such as an operating system, windowing interface, or networking protocol. Open systems, based on industry standards, can be used in any multi-vendor environment, without sacrificing performance, functionality, or the selection of applications and programming tools.

Some will say that the software of an open system must also be portable between different hardware platforms. And on each system to which it is ported, it should be a straightforward process for software engineers to create the same applications.

Some will say that in addition to observing industry standards and providing portability, open systems technologies should promote the following:

- *Interoperability*. The ability of diverse systems to work together.

- *Scalability.* The ability of applications to run on any size system, from a PC to a mainframe.

- *Environment transparency.* The characteristic of the user interface and underlying functionality that makes them appear and operate regardless of the system used.

- *Interface transference.* The empowerment of users that allows them to use their skills on diverse platforms.

All of these are desirable, but they are *not* necessary. The only thing that is necessary for the major business needs is that all components talk and interplay with each other. (They all need the same track gauge.) That standard is, as we have said, 3-tiered, client server, and standards-based (DCE). Any proprietary or "open standard" can operate within this environment.

In the future, we expect another layer, "objects" CORBA on top of DCE, that will allow servers to be objects and communicate with each other using standard objects.

Standards fit into the 3-tiered environments. UNIX, the X Window System, and the Open Software Foundation's DCE are open systems technologies. They can also be considered standards because they have been promulgated as such, most recently by the newest vendor alliance, Cooperative Open Software Environment, known as COSI. Other important open systems standards include POSIX at the operating system level, ANSI C at the programming level, and TCP/IP and NFS at the networking level.

Note that many proprietary environments, such as MVS, AS400, and VMS, have added DCE, thus "opening" them up. *All* environments are "open" in the architecture that we advocate, since they all can inter-operate to solve business problems.

Meanwhile, all these standards need integration with another set of standards—the popular standards on PCs and Macintosh systems. These include Microsoft Windows and the Apple operating system as well as many application-based standards.

With DCE, and with software tools currently available, these two worlds of standards can be melded into one IT solution to business problems and opportunities—thanks to 3-tiered architecture.

The following figure shows how all the "standards" fit into a 3-tiered architecture. The boxes illustrate the three tiers and the list in each box indicates the supporting technologies for communicating between the tiers.

Standards and 3-Tiered Architecture

Presentation Tier	Functionality Tier	Data Tier
MOTIF Windows PM OPENLOOK VT100	DME Version control Security Directory services Startup Shutdown Monitoring Network management Business logic Expert systems	SQL access to relational database SQL access via translator to non-relational data Peer-to-peer: Decnet, LU6.2, TCP/IP sockets Terminal emulation: VT100, 3270

Conclusion

A 3-tiered client-server architecture that separates user interfaces, servers, and data sources provides the foundation on which to build the strategic information applications that can energize and empower your business. Such applications can be built rapidly and modified easily as business circumstances dictate.

Once you have committed to the architecture, the next step is to ensure that the software tools that you employ to build your applications are based on industry-standard open systems. Open systems free you from dependence on any single hardware or software vendor.

First Steps

1. Examine the strategic application(s) that you have selected. Think about ways to separate the application into three tiers (presentation, functionality, and data).

2. Consider ways that you can begin the transition to a 3-tiered client-server architecture. Which legacy systems must be preserved? Which can be replaced, migrated, re-architected?

7

Step 1: Pilot System

"There can and must be harmony between
user and development staff. It can be done now.
Wow!"

> Arnold Holloway, Senior V.P.
> Blue Cross/Blue Shield of Oregon

"Technical people must find a way to give
users what they want. The client-server
technology definitely plays a role in any business
that's looking to level the playing field."

> Ron Cipolla
> Kendall Hospital Supply

"A 3-tiered open systems development
process can help me and my organization break
the systems development log jam."

> Gregory Saffer, Vice President MIS
> Grolion

Executive Summary

You can make an immediate positive impact on
your business by identifying an opportunity to implement your information technology vision. A pilot system can be up and running in one to three weeks when

developed by a Special Weapons and Tactics (SWAT) team using client-server architecture and flexible tools.

This chapter describes the steps used in building a functional pilot system. We believe a pilot system can be built quickly to demonstrate the technical feasibility of a strategic application. This is a necessary precursor to the functionally complete, industrial-strength application.

We advise that you identify the application first, then create a SWAT team (made up of users, managers, and technical staff), build a "greenhouse" to ensure a protected environment, demonstrate the application's technical feasibility, and finally, and very importantly, sell the system. Tell everyone.

Pilot vs. Production

Your staff will design the pilot system in five days or less, and then implement it immediately by taking advantage of the flexibility of the client-server architecture and by using the tools described previously. The pilot system phase is managed by a SWAT team appointed and empowered for this specific task.

It may be hard to believe that any useful system can be developed so quickly, given your past experience with building applications for proprietary architectures. How can anyone build a strategic application, even if it is only a pilot version, in one to two weeks? Consider the alternative: Can you afford to let it take longer? Can you keep users involved in development for more than a week or two? How soon do you need the strategic application on-line, improving your business?

Infrastructure

Note that such development speeds are achievable only after your organization has in place the necessary infrastructure. That infrastructure includes:

- Training personnel in the tools discussed in Appendix A, *Client-Server Tools: Open Environment Corporation*

- Cleaning up the data

- Procuring a network, hardware, and tools

- Developing a process for addressing data integrity

- Ensuring that senior management recognizes the importance of IT

Once you have this infrastructure in place and have used it for yourself, your view of information technology will never be the same.

The rapid development process depends on:

- 3-tiered client-server architecture

- Ease of user interface

- Standard DCE

- Quick compilation/testing cycle

- Tools employing all of the above

- Speacial Weapons and Tactics (SWAT) team

The traditional application-building process is tedious, frustrating, and highly technical. Our one-week, flat-out assault led by non-technical business managers is exciting and highly rewarding. It completely changes the way organizations view information technology.

The pilot system is not an end in itself. It lacks some features necessary for a production application. But do not mistake the pilot system for a "demo" system that you may have built in the past. Everything built in a pilot system can be used in the production application. There is no reason to invest time and money in something you will then throw away. *The pilot systems we are building are functioning applications that tie into live, existing systems.*

Turning the pilot system into a finished production application is a separate process that takes about 10 to 20 weeks. Though developing a production system over several months is phenomenally fast by traditional standards, it is often still too long for daily involvement by users and strategic planners, who are the key to success for any strategic application. Therefore, we build a pilot version first; it then *evolves* into the industrial-strength version of the application.

Building a pilot version accelerates, simplifies, and focuses the development process so that a team of nontechnical managers can construct the most strategic elements of the system in a single week. The pilot system then serves as a detailed outline for the construction of the production system.

Create a SWAT Team

Conventional applications are built by development teams consisting almost entirely of MIS technical people (often hundreds of programmers for a major application). Top organizational managers and system users provide various degrees of input into the process, typically through a "user specifications document," but rarely do such "MIS outsiders" participate directly in building the application.

SWAT development teams differ from application development teams in two important ways:

- SWAT teams consist primarily of organization leaders and system users.
- SWAT teams are much smaller than traditional development teams.

The pilot system architecture allows non-technical people who know the organization's needs to drive the process.

Limiting the number of people on the team is crucial to making a SWAT team effective. Larger groups spend their energy on administrative and political details and rarely retain a strong sense of mission. In addition, the application development process can always encounter unforeseen challenges along the way. Technicians tend to avoid or deny such unanticipated factors as they work toward an unchanging goal. A SWAT team can take advantage of its size and business expertise to overcome unexpected barriers and turn them into strategic opportunities.

Team Membership

Load the team with managers and users. The managers keep the team focused on goals and recognize unforeseen business opportunities as they emerge. Users make sure that the finished application meets their needs and that it is easy to use. When managers and users drive the development process, they feel a sense of ownership and are proud of the finished application.

Not only will they use it, but they will also help sell it to the rest of the organization.

Add technical people. They are crucial to the pilot system SWAT team because they understand the existing systems to which the new application must connect. Having three or four technical people working side-by-side with managers and users is very different from having 250 technical people working on their own. On the SWAT team, technical expertise is directed toward the business needs of the organization and the users.

In addition to technicians, the team must also include two or three people who have had some exposure to the concepts of client-server architecture, either through formal training or prior participation in a similar project. These client-server champions guide the rest of the team's use of the architecture and its tools.

Build a Greenhouse

Once you have identified your SWAT team, you will need to create a "greenhouse" to protect the team from hostile elements and to nurture its growth. Choose isolated facilities to avoid the day-to-day distractions of the office. The team needs to feel a sense of urgency in its mission and needs adequate resources and attention.

Third-party consultants can help provide a fresh viewpoint and can become important members of the team. However, be wary of companies that do not adhere to open systems and ODE tools. Their primary interest may not lie in achieving the goals of *your* organization, but rather in maximizing the sales of *their* organizations and your dependency on them.

It is important to protect the team from cynics in your organization. Many people feel threatened by the changes occurring around them. Protect your SWAT team from such negative responses.

Since selecting a SWAT team is a highly visible process, you run the risk of alienating the rest of your employees by creating a two-class culture. To avoid alienation, rotate your people into and out of the SWAT team. By doing so, you build a bigger team, distribute knowledge and experience more widely, and break down barriers between different groups in your organization.

Demonstrate Technical Feasibility

In five days, your SWAT team can identify, define, and build a pilot version of your strategic application. Check frequently to ensure that the pilot system still matches your organization's goals and critical success factors. The investment in the application thus far has been minimal and chances are you will have a convincing case for proceeding to the production stage.

The technical people work on building the parts of the system behind the user interface (connectivity, databases, data flows, etc.), while users build the actual interface. When your team uses client-server architecture and open systems tools, these pieces can be developed in parallel, with frequent checkpoints between the two efforts. Those tools, critical to the development process, enable users to build interfaces with minimal training and frustration. The interfaces can be modified and tuned rapidly as the users gain experience with the application. Likewise, the technical people use tools that increase their productivity by several orders of magnitude compared to traditional development techniques.

Pilot System Architecture

The pilot system's architecture is identical to that of the production system. The only difference is that the pilot system does not implement every aspect of the production system (cases, functionality, screens, etc.).

Sell the System

At the end of the one- to two-week pilot system development phase, you will have a working pilot system. The pilot demonstrates the primary functions of the target system and connects to your existing system. Demonstrate the pilot system to top management, users, and technical people to gain support for your application.

The pilot system is a valuable tool for "selling" the application. Use it! Emphasize the strategic benefits of the application by showing how the application satisfies organizational goals and critical success factors. Emphasize the difference the application will make to the bottom line. The majority of this information can be drawn from the business case document and included in a one-page executive summary of the business case.

Conclusion

A successful pilot system, developed quickly by non-technical business managers and users in partnership with a small number of technical staff, lays the groundwork for a full-scale production system. The speed of development and user involvement help to excite the user base and empower your personnel. Once you have a functional pilot system, you are ready to develop the full application.

First Steps

1. Identify a SWAT team to develop the strategic application. Select the business leader, user leader, and technical leader.

2. Find a separate physical location to house your "greenhouse."

3. Build your preliminary system, using ODE tools.

4. Refine the business case developed in Chapter 4 using experience gained from the pilot phase.

5. Demonstrate your system to top management and have them buy in and approve the production version.

6. Start placing the needed infrastructure into your organization. Depending on the receptivity of your organization, that infrastructure may take up to one year to implement.

8

Step 2: Production System

"Hamilton Standard has now been able to put the right information at the fingertips of its customers in an easy-to-learn, easy-to-use format."

> Mike Bzullak, Director of Information Technology
> Hamilton Standard

"We place large value on our current managed health care system and do not want to replace it. The OEC open systems concept allows us to add new functions to the current system and still maintain its core features without replacing it in its entirety."

> Larry Rivers, Director of Health Plan Systems
> United HealthCare

"Our major information concern is to create an interrelated enterprise-wide architecture that interfaces smoothly with our largest customers so that we can manage a paperless business in a cost efficient manner to meet all of the needs of our customers and our employees."

> John A. Vivash, President and CEO
> CIBC Securities, Inc.

Executive Summary

Build on your successful pilot system to deploy an industrial-strength application that gives strategic advantage to your business. Using client-server architecture, open systems tools, and the SWAT team approach, production systems take 10 to 20 weeks to implement, rather than one to six years with traditional architectures and techniques.

A strategic system is a living, changing entity that evolves to meet the organization's dynamic needs, creates new business opportunities, and helps your organization stay ahead of competitors.

Client-server architecture gives you two long-term options for implementing systems:

- New systems can be built from scratch.

- Old applications and data can be expanded and restructured gradually, as new applications in your open systems architecture absorb and replace the existing systems.

Once you have deployed your production system, network management becomes a strategic issue.

Building the System

It is time to build a powerful, complete, industrial-strength version of the application you created in the pilot system phase. The production system takes 10 to 20 weeks to complete. If that seems long, compare it to the traditional approach.

Development Time: Traditional vs. Client-Server

Phase	Traditional Approach	Client-Server Approach
Feasibility	Prototype: 1 to 6 months	Pilot System: 1 to 3 weeks
Final User Specifications	1 to 6 months	(Continuous)
System Design	3 months to 1 year	(Included in Pilot System)
Coding	6 months to 3 years	Production System: 9 to 20 weeks
Testing & Revision	3 months to 1 year for most changes	(Continuous. 1 week for most changes.)
Total Time:	**1 to 6 years**	**10 to 20 weeks**

There is a big difference between the time required to build applications using traditional and client-server development methods.

Remember, traditional "demos" are limited programs that simulate the required functionality of a very simple application. Traditional demos cannot tie together two similar systems running on the same computer, much less a half-dozen dissimilar systems running on different computers. The best an MIS department can do with traditional development techniques is attempt to incorporate some of the prototype's functionality into the production version. The new pilot system, on the other hand, is a sophisticated (albeit no-frills) version of the production system that is functional from the outset.

The Development Process

The process of building a production system parallels that of building a pilot system. You use the same application architecture and add robustness. The production system architecture, like the pilot system architecture, eliminates the long and difficult process of developing a system architecture from scratch. The architecture consists of modules that need only be customized to provide the capabilities required for the strategic application. These modules are more sophisticated than their pilot counterparts, and they provide a higher level of performance, functionality, and flexibility.

The SWAT team approach for production systems is similar to the pilot system approach. A small, highly focused team of users, managers, and technical experts customizes a set of tools. Of course, building the production system requires more time and technical expertise.

Transforming a pilot system into a production system is more than a trivial exercise. Let's look at an actual pilot system and see what enhancements were required to turn it into a production system.

A Sample System

A major airline built a pilot system, linking its inventory, scheduling, and maintenance systems in one week. Developing its production system took 28 weeks.

The following table compares the features of the two systems.

Pilot vs. Production

Pilot System Features	Production System Features
Updates inventory in 10 seconds	Updates inventory in <1 second
Supports two users	Supports entire worldwide org.
Assumes part numbers	Verifies part numbers with user
Allows access by anyone	Verifies user identity
Does not handle errors	Handles errors
Contains limited functions	Contains all functions
Does not provide maintenance or network management	Provides full maintenance and network management
Developed in 3 weeks	Developed in 20 weeks
Hardware platform irrelevant	Hardware platform determined

Performance Issues

The production system must provide high performance and fast response time if it is to offer mission-critical services. Some performance improvements occur automatically when new tools and system modules replace their pilot system counterparts. If the computer hardware is slow, portions of the application can be ported to a larger computer or distributed among multiple computers to boost performance. The client-server architecture actually encourages such distribution of the computing load.

In some cases, response time suffers as a result of outside systems beyond the team's control. Bringing the outside systems into the client-server environment to operate as part of the data processing module can reduce such delays. Although this may not be an immediate concern, the team should consider enveloping the outside system in the future.

Many performance-enhancement products for the 3-tiered client-server environment are now appearing on the market. For example, IBM has announced a transaction processing CICS for this architecture. Transarc has announced ENCINA. Unisys has announced TUXEDO. These transaction monitors also automate the two-phase commit issue.

Further performance gains are possible when you distribute multiple copies of a server onto several machines to provide parallel processing.

Project Management

Maintain user involvement throughout the project. Checking in with your key users is vital to success. Measure your team's effectiveness using evaluation forms that rate user satisfaction with the application as development proceeds. The evaluations also help you substantiate your success or highlight substantive problems that you need to correct. Should problems arise, OEC and other companies provide many tools to help manage these environments.

Pilot Test

As production system development nears completion, components must be tested and integrated. When the entire application is functional, you can begin the pilot test phase. The pilot test puts a few users on the system in a controlled environment, allowing them to identify bugs and make recommendations before the system is fully deployed. Critical day-to-day operations are unaffected by such testing.

Continuous Improvement

Even if the system is living up to its strategic promise, you cannot assume that it is a finished product. Three things will happen:

- The strategic needs of the organization will change.
- The users of the system will discover new requirements.
- The competitive environment will change.

You must be committed to a process of continuous improvement in each of your strategic applications if you are to meet the challenge of such changing circumstances. Fortunately, modifying and enhancing a strategic application is far easier with client-server architecture than with more traditional approaches. You can add new interfaces and functionality easily, without rewriting existing programs. You can incorporate users' suggestions in a few days or weeks by changing or adding servers without interrupting your operations. You can attach additional databases to your application in hours by plugging in new server modules, and you can build entirely new databases in a matter of days, all without stopping operations.

To take maximum advantage of the client-server architecture's ability to meet the changing needs of users and organizations, be sure that people are looking for new opportunities. Bring the managers and SWAT team members involved in the original project together once a week for a few months, and once a month thereafter to keep people involved.

Security

Security is a key feature of the DCE environment. In this environment, you can use security servers, such as MIT's Kerberos. As various proprietary systems become DCE-compliant, you can ensure single-point security management of your entire distributed environment.

Version Control

In the 3-tiered client-server architecture, version control servers can be written to take action when the DCE mechanisms detect a version mismatch.

Goals and CSFs Revisited

Follow-up teams should review the goals and critical success factors that defined the original strategic application idea. The teams can determine if the goals have changed or if new goals are emerging. With new goals in hand, the teams can identify the relevant critical success factors; formulate ideas for adapting or enhancing the re-engineered processes; and enhance the IT implementation of the application to reflect the business changes.

For example, the goal of the nearly bankrupt Chrysler organization was survival in the 1980s, and a critical success factor was maintaining cash flow, hence the process of tracking cash. If Chrysler had decided to build a strategic application to address this critical success factor, it might have applied client-server architecture to its dealership and supplier accounting systems to determine its cash, accounts receivable, and accounts payable on any given day. A few months later,

Chrysler's new goal was market share, so the primary critical success factor became improving the quality of its cars. To adapt the strategic system to this new critical success factor, the company might have added a defect-tracking database to its dealership and supplier connections.

Application Evolution

As an organization continues to modify and expand an application, it may eventually make sense to restructure the application and replace the original systems. The original systems may no longer offer adequate performance or flexibility. In other instances, the client-server application grows around the original systems, isolating them into a relatively small part of the larger application.

In either case, client-server architecture gives an organization two options: Leave the original standard systems intact or restructure the environment to absorb and replace the existing systems.

The flexibility of client-server architecture makes the latter option the wiser choice, especially when the architecture already incorporates most of the application. However, some organizations' MIS departments are too committed to traditional technologies to allow the transition to a new environment, regardless of the advantages. These organizations can use client-server architecture as a strategic bridge between original and new applications. The new environment and the original systems can be replaced piece-by-piece using conventional technologies until a new, integrated application is in place.

In many cases, evolving organizational goals require you to develop a separate application rather than to modify or expand an existing strategic application. To ensure that your organization recognizes such opportunities and allows strategic applications to realize their full potential, you must institutionalize the necessary attitudes, methodologies, and technologies. But first we must examine the crucial challenge of managing strategic computer networks.

Managing the Strategic Network

One consequence of embracing a client-server architecture for strategic information systems is the increased importance of computer networking. Networks provide the communications backbone for distributed applications. In traditional architectures, applications run on a single machine; network failures are usually a nuisance but nothing more. But with client-server architecture, network failures can mean the difference between life and death.

"Our network must never go down, not just for competitive reasons, but because the health of people is at stake."

Maribeth Luftglass, Associate Director
Telecommunications
American Red Cross

"I think that sharing the concepts, knowledge, and experience [of strategic networks] will significantly influence the way I approach both my professional and personal life for many years to come."

Larry Shuford, Director IT Services
Department of Natural Resources
State of Colorado

Network management is thus transformed from being a tactical issue to being an issue of strategic importance. Fortunately, robust, proven solutions have recently become available.

Network management deals with three levels of hardware and software:

- *The physical level.* If modems, cables, and other communications hardware components fail, you must manage that failure by rerouting the information around the failed components.

- *The system level.* If computer systems in the network become overloaded, you must redistribute the computing load. Can you monitor the performance of every machine on the network? This is a *system-level* management question.

- *The application level.* What happens if the data transmission is flawless and the computing performance is fine, but someone changes one of the applications or modules that your application depends on for data? What if the data changes its format on a remote system? These are *application-level* questions.

The following sections briefly discuss the issues at each level.

The Physical Level

Network components that can fail at the physical level include telephone lines, modems, and communications controllers. There are products designed to monitor these components and alert network administrators when a component fails. Tools such as AT&T's Dataphone II and IBM's NetView help diagnose physical component problems.

The vendors of communications and network hardware produce highly reliable equipment. Even though you may install security equipment, we suspect that you will find the failure rate low.

The System Level

Monitoring computer systems for performance overload can be accomplished using such vendor-supplied tools as NetView (for IBM environments) and DECnet (for DEC environments). Organizations that have 3-tiered client-server environments built with OEC tools can monitor their environments using Net-Minder, which is included as part of the OEC Run-Time library.

The Application Level

You have built and deployed a client-server application to gain a strategic advantage. What is the likelihood that some customer, some supplier, some division, or some other entity on the network will make a change that affects your application? The answer is, "100%." Take the Bank of Boston as an example. The Bank introduces an average of 250 application software changes *every week*. What happens to your interface when some independent supplier on the network changes its application? Conventional network management tools offer no means to cope with such alterations.

The Traditional Solution to Application Changes

The traditional strategy for avoiding unexpected changes is to dictate a policy to all organizations capable of modifying any part of the system. You might decree, for example, "Anyone who makes a change to the system without prior notification and approval will be shot on sight."

Such policies are fundamentally inappropriate to today's strategic applications networks. First of all, it is unlikely that one organization controls an entire strategic network: Customers, suppliers, and users all contribute to the network, and the lines between "user" and "owner" have become increasingly blurred. If the user responsible for making a change to "your" network is a customer, what do you do? When changes occur to applications on which your systems depend, what happens?

The Client-Server Solution to Application Changes

Standards are now being set to manage distributed applications. One example is OEC tools such as NetMinder, which is based on the concepts in the Distributed Management Environment (DME) from the Open Software Foundation.

The modular design of client-server architecture allows swift modifications to the special servers (or "filters") that translate information between systems. Because these filters are extremely compact, modifications can be made in minutes.

Another challenge is identifying which servers need to be altered for a given application change. To meet that need, it is possible to construct a "server table" server for your client-server applications, which automatically finds the servers affected by a particular change. In conventional environments, finding and fixing a function could take weeks, if it could be accomplished at all.

In the future, expert systems will detect changes automatically and make the required corrections. Test versions of such expert systems exist today and are being incorporated into client-server applications around the world.

Installing the correct strategic network management solution is crucial if you are to harness the full benefits of strategic information technology. There is no last step; there is no end date. An organization must be committed to continuous refinements in order to maintain strategic advantage.

The Client-Server
Network Management Architecture

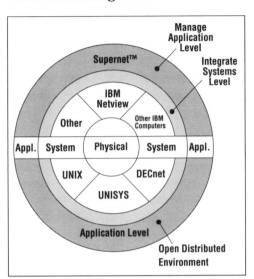

Conclusion

By building on the success of your pilot system, you can create an industrial-strength production system in an amazingly short period of time. Once the application is built and deployed, you can use appropriate network management tools to ensure that the network provides new strategic benefits to your organization.

First Steps

1. Direct the SWAT team to design the production system based on the pilot system; write a detailed project plan.

2. Re-evaluate your strategic application. Does it still meet the goals and critical success factors of the organization? Does your business case justify taking it to production?

3. Create a forum so that users and technical staff can evaluate the production application on an ongoing basis. Designate resources for continuous improvement of the application.

4. Determine your long-term strategy for the application. Do you want the client-server environment to absorb your existing systems?

5. Use physical-level network management tools to service your physical network management needs.

6. Use system-level network management tools to manage each of your systems properly.

7. Integrate these systems to produce a comprehensive and consistent user interface for heterogeneous system-level network management.

8. Install tools to detect and alert the network manager to applications changes.

9

New Ground:
Meeting the Challenge of Change

"Management of change is the common thread that will ultimately determine your success . . . Change is all too often cast negatively. We need to find ways to use change positively to further our goals."

Bernie Gorman, Deputy Comptroller
Canadian Federal Government

"There are profound changes in the marketplace we serve. We must change rapidly and dramatically or face poor to mediocre performance."

Mike Tallert, President and CEO
Lone Star Gas Company

Executive Summary

The client-server architecture brings changes to the operation of your MIS department and promotes a new perspective on the role of an organization's Chief Executive Officer (CEO) and Chief Information Officer (CIO). It also brings changes to traditional relationships with technology vendors. Managing those changes effectively is a critical challenge.

New Roles for MIS and the CIO

For 20 years, the MIS function and an organization's CIO have been concerned with centralizing the data processing operation.[1] The "old days" of comfortable, centralized computer systems are gone. Several forces are driving computing and communications toward decentralization:

- Strategic applications tend to tie together systems in organizations over which the CIO has no control (such as suppliers and customers).

- Users bring specialized computers into their offices. These computers are so inexpensive that they can be hidden in the department's budget!

- Mergers and acquisitions bring new systems into the fold.

- Customized systems are easily developed on small machines, but may require connections to data residing on other systems.

- Software development productivity is higher on small machines for many applications.

- Small, decentralized machines may be a more economical way of distributing computing power among users.

- New processor technologies (such as parallel processors) may have to be integrated with existing systems.

---

[1]For a detailed discussion of the changing role of the CIO, see John J. Donovan, "Beyond Chief Information Officer to Network Manager," *Harvard Business Review*, Sept.-Oct. 1988.

There is no way to stop these changes from happening. How will these changes impact your organization, and how can you minimize their disruptive effect?

Some portion of your data processing may always be centralized, but it is inevitable that some component will be decentralized. Hence, the fundamental role of the CIO is changing. The CIO is becoming more strategic, more concerned with the network, and less concerned with the day-to-day operation of the computers.

Technical Changes—Opportunity or Crisis?

When steam-powered ships were first introduced, what was the reaction of the sailing industry? They refused to accept the technological change, instead adding larger sails and more masts to their fleets. The enhanced sailing vessel, although faster than its predecessor, failed to match the power and speed of the engine-driven vessel. Ultimately, sailing vessels used for commercial purposes died. The sailing industry had missed a strategic advantage and an opportunity.

Changing information technology is now challenging organizations in similar ways. You must take advantage of technological changes, including:

- Tactical batch systems that are evolving to strategic on-line applications

- Closed, centralized systems that are yielding to a new world of connectivity and open architectures

- Decision-support functions that are being replaced by expert systems that actually *make* decisions

- Traditional computers that are being challenged by parallel processors providing 100 times more processing speed

Single-vendor influence in organizations is giving way to multi-vendor architectures with the advent and acceptance of open systems standards. Are you going to convince your organization to adapt to the new technologies and lead the new generation of information technology, or are you going to construct bigger sails and more masts?

A Strategy for Managing Change

With adequate foresight and preparation, you can address and neutralize all of your organization's impediments to change. Here are eight specific actions you can take to overcome them:

- Share your vision.

- Understand and manage the change curve.

- Forestall defensiveness and threats.

- Avoid bureaucracy.

- Combat envy.

- Provide a support structure for change.

- Avoid the crabs.

- Get people involved.

Share Your Vision

As a senior officer of your organization, you have a vision for your organization and a method for implementing those goals. How do you enlist support for your vision?

Give your people structure. For thousands of years, humans saw fossils in rocks throughout the world. It was not until Darwin's Theory of Evolution that people realized what the fossils were. Darwin gave them structure.

Never miss an opportunity to present your vision. There will always be some analogy that can make people see what you mean. With the strategic applications we have discussed here, live demonstrations give people a structure and present opportunities for the advocates to explain their vision over and over again.

Understand and Manage the Change Curve

When people are asked to undertake a project that involves changing attitudes and routines, their level of enthusiasm and confidence goes through a fairly predictable evolution. At the start of the project, enthusiasm is extremely high and, thanks to the new approach, overwhelming success seems inevitable. But as soon as the project starts running into its first snags and setbacks, massive disillusionment replaces the initial confidence, and now failure seems likely. As problems get solved, the project team gradually rebuilds its enthusiasm to a more realistic level.

The danger in this roller coaster ride of emotions is that the project will suffer irreparable damage as people reach the stage where confidence plummets. Two things can be done to minimize the problem. First, the leader can *reduce unrealistic expectations* by anticipating some of the problems that the group is likely to encounter. Second, the team leader can *keep the team focused on its goals* rather than letting the team wallow in the discouraging details of temporary problems. It is crucial at this stage to keep everything stable, routine, and predictable; people already on unfamiliar territory may be tempted to revert to older approaches when faced with additional changes or surprises.

It is important to realize that managers are often ahead of their employees on the change curve, hitting peaks and valleys earlier than everyone else. Keep this in mind. Explain the curve and what to expect to the other team members. Openness is the best way to eliminate suspicion.

Forestall Defensiveness and Threats

Defensiveness impairs a person's ability to see the need for change, much less act on it. New technologies like client-server architecture are threatening to both your employees and your vendors. How do you thwart defensiveness so that people can react to change?

Focus everyone on the goals of the organization. Keep them from dwelling on their personal "fiefs" and fears. Defensiveness and threats can be minimized by keeping people goal-oriented and by moving the application development process along quickly.

Avoid Bureaucracy

Keep it moving. Many organizations have established lengthy and cumbersome processes to review and approve each stage of application development. This process is acceptable with the lengthy development of tactical applications, but it can kill development of a strategic application. Subjecting a three-month project to a six-month review process will stop the project's momentum, dampen enthusiasm, and burden the process with unnecessary or damaging changes. Lengthy reviews result in missed opportunities.

If an application SWAT team is in danger of stalling, seek higher-level approval to circumvent corporate policy and to continue with the project.

Combat Envy

Envy—the wish to destroy those who are perceived as having "more"—is a serious problem and can easily arise if SWAT team members, for example, are perceived as better than everyone else.

It is a good idea to channel overly competitive feelings away from the job. One solution is to form user groups in which people affected by new, existing, or proposed systems meet on a regular basis to provide direct input to development teams. These groups broaden the base of people in the organization who contribute to the new application. These individuals then act as change agents for the rest of the organization.

You can move people into the strategic applications process continually. When a SWAT team has accomplished a highly visible and successful project and is about to start another, it is a good time to form more SWAT teams. A single SWAT team can be perceived as elitist, while multiple SWAT teams increase the number of people involved with the project.

Provide a Support Structure for Change

SWAT teams do best in an environment designed to nourish creativity and innovation. Just as it is necessary to create the proper environment when building the pilot system, it is also important to keep this environment for long-term projects.

Building an infrastructure within the organization is important, but convincing senior executives to support the projects is critical. *Top management should see demonstrations first.* Support from the CEO is helpful, but a broad range of support among top management is more dependable than the support of one key executive.

Avoid the Crabs

"Crabs" are the people who prevent you from doing new things. If you recognize them early, you may be able to change their attitudes before they cause any great damage. If you cannot convince them to reform, you should isolate or remove them.

Remember, crabs can only move sideways and backwards, never forward. Crabs will always try to hold back those who climb toward the top of the basket. You can recognize them by their lack of constructive criticisms or alternatives.

Get People Involved

Many other tools for managing change can be applied to the transition to strategic information technology. It is important that managers recognize that change is difficult for everyone, and that people need to have some control over change. Your best ideas are doomed to failure if you thrust them upon people without considering the needs of those individuals first. If these needs are accounted for, people's attitudes will reinforce rather than pull against the power of the new approaches. *People, not technologies or methodologies, will determine the success of efforts to make information more strategic in an organization.*

Conclusion

Making the transition to client-server architecture brings change throughout your organization, starting with the CIO and extending to your technology suppliers. You can deal effectively with people's reactions to change by recognizing their needs and clearly articulating your vision. And you can manage your vendors by relying on the competition created by open systems.

First Steps

1. Provide a structure and model of the vision you have for your employees. Keep everyone goal-oriented and insist that all projects address corporate goals. Goal orientation gives people a structure for grasping your corporate vision, keeps them from being defensive, and helps them through the inevitable change-curve slumps.

2. Form small user groups within your organization. These groups allow people to participate in decisions regarding the changes they will have to face, and this increases their sense of control.

3. Manage the change curve and train managers to do the same. Managers should set everyone's expectations appropriately at the outset of a new

133

project, and should discuss the change curve with their employees to prepare them for what lies ahead.

4. Watch out for crabs. If you recognize them early, you may be able to change their attitudes before they cause any great damage. If you cannot convince them to reform, you should isolate or remove them.

5. Technological innovations drive down the cost of information components at a rapid rate. To take advantage of improved price/performance, choose solutions based on open systems standards for computing and communications. Competition among open systems vendors brings the best values.

10

A Look Ahead: Technology Weapons of the Future

"Who's lined up at the door [of MIT's Media Lab]? The business studs . . . Their interest is simple: They want to stay in business, and if the business environment shifts, they have got to shift with it, preferably just ahead of it."

Stewart Brand, *The Media Lab: Inventing the Future at MIT*

"Identify the trends/directions and what is available."

Takashi Kiuchi, Chairman and CEO
Mitsubishi Electronics America

"We need to understand our customers, the marketplace, and the technologies in order to be able to add value as well as solutions to our customers' business problems."

Patty Johnson
IBM

"My main IT concern is to be able to identify new technology options that can move our market position further in the fast changing environment."

Anders Broman, Marketing Manager
GB Glace AB Sweden

Executive Summary

Consider four emerging technologies for inclusion in your arsenal of weapons: object technology, expert systems, computers capable of parallel processing, and new techniques for user interfaces. These technologies are available today and will be even more powerful in the future. They can improve the power and usefulness of your information systems.

- *Object technology*: Allows you to activate, interchange, and modify objects (data and functions) around a network, and provides significant productivity gains in software engineering through reusable code.

- *Expert systems:* Allow you to capture the experience of your best employees and extend their knowledge throughout the organization.

- *Parallel processing computers:* Give you a competitive edge in time-critical, computationally intensive applications.

- *New technologies for user interfaces*: Expand your user base and promote more effective use of information resources.

These technologies can be integrated smoothly and economically with your existing systems using client-server architecture when you use ODE tools.

Object Technology

Object-oriented computing represents the next wave in the future of software development. The use of object technology will significantly increase programmer productivity and improve program maintainability. It actually represents an entirely new way of thinking about software.

Programs comprise "objects" that may be data or software functions. Those objects have properties associated with them and they can pass those properties along to other objects. Best of all, programs can be constructed quickly by reusing existing objects in new ways (rather than reinventing a function every time you need it).

We suggest that you start your IT department down the object technology path, perhaps by investing in object-oriented user interface tools such as the Object Power C++ Presentation Toolkits available on PCs and workstations.

Once objects are in place, the next step is to get on the tier, to start using 3-tiered client-server architecture with objects.

Where to start? Start with the interfaces (e.g., Object Power has developed an object-oriented GUI). Starting here will get people using new systems and buying in to the new method of computing.

Many Black Boxes

If you are a senior manager, you know that black boxes are the crown jewels of any organization. (A "box" performs some function, such as your accounting department.) The 3-tiered approach is chockfull of black boxes. And, in a large sense, it is a black box it-self—providing an overall computing solution, without forcing a proprietary technology on the organization.

Why the black box comparison? Objects are black boxes.

Consider this: The sophisticated black boxes that are standard equipment on every commercial airline provide FAA information gatherers with answers. These information gatherers are unaware of the technology inside; they are only concerned with the flight recorder data and other readings.

Clients and servers will evolve to objects. In fact, using tools presently being developed, your servers will be able to be recompiled into CORBA-compliant objects.

Anatomy of an Object

What exactly is an object? An object is an internal structure, such as a program. Moreover, an object has a known set of operations.

This set of operations may increase or decrease depending on how dynamic the object. The degree of an object's dynamic capabilities depends, in large part, on the number of other objects helping it define its set of operations. Think of these objects as active objects, objects that in some way affect anything outside of themselves.

Objects are also passive. They execute their set of operations on themselves. They do not actively parse data and spew forth results. Instead, the presence of a certain type of data causes an object to react according to its instructions, which then causes another object to get involved. The processing ends when the final object in the chain communicates some piece of information to the user.

Expert Systems

Expert systems attempt to model the judgment of human experts by representing the expert's decision-making techniques using a collection of "if-then" rules. Although the expert systems concept has been in vogue since the mid-1980s, such systems have not yet made significant inroads into strategic business applications. Why aren't expert systems more common?

There are three factors that make implementing expert systems a difficult process:

- Expert systems work well only for certain types of problems—those that can be solved by strict application of "if-then" rules. Thus expert systems cannot be applied to every task in an organization.

- Certain technical considerations must be met to make a given expert system feasible and worthwhile.

- Expert systems must be able to extract data from the organization's existing computer systems.

Automating the Judgments of Experts

Expert systems work well in areas where "judgment calls" are important to business activities. For example, you might wish to capture the expertise of the best salespeople in your telemarketing organization and make that expertise available to the entire staff.

Through questioning and observation, professional "knowledge engineers" can transform the decision-making process of the best salespeople into a set of "if-then" rules. When less successful salespeople apply these rules to their own situations, their performance improves dramatically.

A simple financial decision-support tool, using expert system technology, might take information about an individual (such as income, marital status, and debt burden) as input, apply a set of rules, and then recommend the proper mix of savings accounts, checking accounts, and certificates of deposit to match the individual's investment profile.

Expert systems make an expert's judgment and experience available to a wide range of people. To identify an area that might be suitable for an expert system application, ask the following questions. If the answer to each one is "yes," then the expert system application can be built.

1. Can you *identify experts* at this job?

2. Is there a *specialized body of knowledge and experience* that enables the experts to do this job well?

3. Is this specialized knowledge at the right stage of development (if not yet an exact science, at least not a "black art")?

4. Are the experts *capable of articulating their knowledge*? (Doing so involves enduring a lengthy interview process.)

5. Does the knowledge involve *a chain of reasoning*—a sequential process of intermediate "decisions" that eventually lead to a conclusion?

After establishing technical feasibility, estimate the cost and payoff of the system. Development cost varies with the number of decision rules the system employs. Systems of moderate complexity (400 or fewer rules) can be reasonably priced and highly useful. Such systems have a relatively flat cost curve: They should cost between $50,000 and $100,000 to develop. Costs rise much more steeply as the complexity of the system increases.

You can calculate the benefits of the proposed system by estimating the value of one-half the difference in performance between your experts and non-experts. This is approximately what the expert system will produce in improved decision-making performance.

Implementation of the Expert System

The expert system is implemented as a server in the middle tier. By using available tools, you can implement it in any language (e.g., C, OPS, LISP, etc.).

An expert system embodies the best judgment of your employees, but without access to the best information, the system will never achieve its full potential. Chances are that the necessary information already exists on the computers within your organization. You need a quick link between this information and the new expert system.

Client-server architecture can provide a reliable, flexible way of getting the data from existing systems into the new expert system application. There is no need to modify your existing systems or change the expert system every time you want to use data from an additional source. The new, expert system becomes one more server integrated with your other information systems in a strategic network.

Parallel Processing Computers

Parallel processing computers can be used in a 3-tiered architecture to run servers or data servers. They give you tremendous computing power for situations in which speed is critical. There are parallel processing computers on the market today that are *two orders of magnitude faster than the quickest conventional machines*. If computing were traveling, this speed difference would make the flight from New York to Los Angeles last three minutes instead of six hours!

Parallel processing computers are faster and more economical than conventional machines. Instead of doing all of the work on one expensive processor, the job is divided among simpler, linked processors that work concurrently.

The challenge lies in finding applications that can fully exploit multiple processors, and in integrating the new hardware with your existing information systems.

Finding the Right Applications

Does your need for high-speed processing mean that you must wait for ever-faster single-processor machines? Not necessarily. You can boost processing speed dramatically whenever a task can be broken down into more than one parallel subtask. For example, if you wanted to search 4,000 libraries for all documents relating to oil refining, you could assign a single serial processing computer to search each library in sequence. But with parallel processing, you could assign *4,000 processors* to search each library *concurrently*, reducing search time by a factor of 4,000!

And parallel processing machines offer high speed using conventional technology. Their high speed comes from a large number of identical, off-the-shelf components (like CPU chips and memory), and so their cost rises linearly with performance. By adding more processors, *it is possible to get a parallel processing computer customized for virtually any speed and cost requirements.*

Parallel processing computers are available today from a variety of vendors and continue to evolve rapidly.

Integrating Parallel Processing with Your Existing Environment

Parallel processing computers provide unprecedented computing power for accelerating critical applications. Can you integrate this new type of equipment with your existing systems?

To maximize its usefulness, the parallel processing computer has to receive information from, and return results to, the other applications running on your existing systems. Moving all of your applications to parallel processing machines is unrealistic and unnecessary. *Client-server architecture lets you link the parallel processing machine and its time-critical applications to your existing applications with minimal effort and disruption.*

143

Integrating Old and New Processing Technologies

User Interface Technologies

Can your employees understand and fully exploit their computing tools to perform their jobs? *User interfaces are the key to using information systems effectively.*

Conventional User Interfaces Are Primitive

Have you ever talked to a person who showed no facial expression and who neither agreed nor disagreed with what you were saying? It was painful and unsettling, wasn't it? What was wrong?

The problem with such interactions is that they provide one-way communication. In similar fashion,

144

computers today give little positive reinforcement during their interactions with users. They neither grunt, nor speak, nor nod their monitors in agreement.

Conventional interfaces between human users and their computers are terrible. Years of experience have conditioned us to expect only the most primitive interactions with our computing tools. This is not only tragic, but completely unnecessary.

The Situation Is Improving

The days of dumb terminals with their mesmerizing rows of lime green characters are numbered. Graphical user interfaces, such as those provided by X Windows, Microsoft Windows, and the Macintosh operating system, expand display capabilities to include graphs, technical drawings, photographs, and even full-motion, interactive video, all at ever-diminishing costs. Even they will become old hat with the availability of multimedia technologies.

The advent of graphical user interface design tools is an interesting phenomenon in the three major markets that compete in the presentation layer of the 3-tiered architecture.

In both the UNIX and Microsoft Windows markets, there are numerous products that support their native platform. On the UNIX side, these include UIM/X from Visual Edge, XFaceMaker from Non Standard Logics, and Builder Xccessory from Integrated Computer Solutions. On the Microsoft Windows side, you have such products as Visual Basic, Toolbook, Oracle Card, Enfin, and Powerbuilder. (Note: Do not use Oracle Card, Powerbuilder, or a similar software package in its 2-tiered mode. It will trap you and limit your organization.)

Non-visual interfaces are also emerging. Apple Computer and others have announced voice recognition systems, such as the one used in the Newton, that can recognize large vocabularies of continuous speech from untrained users. Systems such as these will become clients in the 3-tiered architecture.

The future will be with multimedia interfaces that you can use to gather data from multiple computing sessions running in various windows on your computer screen. You can then *share* that data with colleagues in London and Tokyo *in real time*. You can see their faces on your screen as, together, you highlight items of concern in the data and discuss it among yourselves. You can talk to your computer and it will talk back. This capability exists today.

Conclusion

Object technology, expert systems, parallel processing machines, and new user interface techniques can be potent additions to your technology arsenal. Used judiciously, they can improve the power and usefulness of your information systems. And by applying client-server architecture to your strategic applications, you can integrate these technologies smoothly and economically with your existing systems.

First Steps

1. Implement object technology in your software system now.

2. Is expert judgment of paramount importance in your organization? Where would more informed, consistent decision-making produce the

greatest value? Answer the five feasibility questions earlier in this chapter, and produce a cost-benefit analysis for each potential application.

3. Identify instances where processing speed is critical. Does the processing power of your existing systems create a bottleneck? Start experimenting with a parallel processing machine.

4. Investigate new user interface technologies like touch-screens, video, multimedia, and speech peripheral hardware. Could new user interfaces based on such devices improve access to critical systems? Identify opportunities to apply client-server architecture to existing applications that might take advantage of new user interfaces.

11

Conclusion:
A Call to Action

"We must make it happen in a coordinated
and consistent way quickly. We must not be ob-
sessed by cost. This will be difficult. We must not
be deflected from our vision."

Ralph Kugler, Chairman
Lever Brothers Malaysia

"We want to leverage our worldwide presence
and diversity competitively."

Timothy J. Leveque, President
ALCOA

Congratulations! You have completed an important
educational experience, and you are now prepared to
apply the client-server model to your organization's information architecture to gain strategic advantage in today's competitive markets.

The democratization of technology brought about
by the open systems revolution places new tools in the
hands of the people who need it most. The approach described in this book frees your organization from being
held hostage by competitive forces and outdated
technologies.

Knowledge is critical, but not sufficient. You must
act on that knowledge to make a difference in your

organization. The opportunities—and the tools—are available to all.

Be a winner. Seize the opportunity to make your new vision of information systems a strategic reality for your organization.

First Steps

1. Identify a strategic application.

2. Develop a business case.

3. Form a SWAT team.

4. Create a "to do" list:

   a. Identify applications to be right-sized.
   b. Identify strategic applications to be built.
   c. Implement an IT policy to convert all applications to a 3-tiered, standards-based architecture.

5. Pick a positive environment (or "greenhouse") suitable for both users and technologists to implement your first application.

6. Manage the change and continue to add value to your strategic applications.

7. Do it NOW—don't let the crabs get you.

Appendix A
Client-Server Tools, An Example:
Open Environment Corporation

You have seen how to gain strategic business benefits by taking advantage of the 3-tiered client-server architecture. This section discusses a set of software tools developed specifically to support application development for this architecture. This set of software tools is offered by the Open Environment Corporation (OEC). OEC was founded in order to make development of the 3-tiered client-server architecture quicker and easier. Today OEC Toolkits are being used worldwide. They are available from all major vendors for major hardware platforms and operating systems.

Empowering Your Organization

Numerous organizations are now using these OEC tools to their advantage. What are these tools, what are the standards, and how did distributed client-server technology fit into the current computing strategy of these organizations?

Standards

Open Software Foundation (OSF) has specified the standards for an open, object-distributed computing environment. One key standard is the Common Object Request Broker (CORBA), built on such standards as the Distributed Computing Environment (DCE).

These standards include:

- A method for applications to communicate with each other through remote procedure calls (RPC)

- A method of keeping track of clients and servers through "naming services" or "brokers"

- A security mechanism, Kerberos

- Application Environment Standards (AES)

- A Distributed Management Environment (DME) for managing the environment

OEC has developed tools to facilitate the development of applications that utilize these standards.

Capabilities of the Open Environment Corporation

OEC provides a set of application development tools that allow you to utilize today's hardware and software in a 3-tiered client-server environment. To achieve this end, OEC Toolkits provide services in five general categories:

- *Basic services*. These provide standard services that are not yet supplied by platform vendors, such as naming services on MPE brokers on VMS.

- *Bridges.* This allows existing tools like Oracle and Visual Basic to communicate with the basic services.

- *Code generation and application development services.* These provide procedure code for both client and server.

- *Application management services.* These provide standard functions such as version control, startup, shutdown, and monitoring.

- *Connectivity and database servers.* These tools generate servers that can access or update data.

Basic Services

By definition, every client-server architecture has some method of sending information between clients and servers. The 3-tiered client-server architecture of OEC uses a standard client-server communications mechanism to achieve this end. RPC technology is one of the standards that enables programmers to distribute application modules across various machines in a network, depending on the capabilities of each machine. In its simplest form, an application might consist of a user interface module on a desktop PC (client), and an information providing program (server). RPC standards allow a program on the PC to activate the server simply by calling it remotely.

RPC technology allows two modules to behave as though they both resided on the same machine. It shields application developers from the complexities of

underlying network technologies, and allows developers to move, modify, replace, replicate, group, and mix-
and-match clients and servers running across diverse
hardware and software with no changes to the client
and server programs. Servers perform services for any
interested client, while their locations and implementation details are transparent to all clients and handled by
the name services.

Open Environment Corporation's OEC tools were
developed before an industry-standard, client-server
communications mechanism was available on all machines. The initial releases of OEC (1.0 and 1.1) use the
OEC RPC library, a flexible mechanism which con-
sumes little CPU time. Later releases of OEC (2.x and
above) allow developers to use the industry standard
RPC mechanisms provided by the Distributed Computing Environment (DCE) from the Open Software
Foundation.

As each platform vendor introduces its own implementation of the basic services, applications built with
OEC tools will migrate automatically.

Bridges

In the near term, DCE applications are appearing in
all industries, especially aerospace, universities, businesses with heavy network demands, and banking.
Close on the heels of these are applications for network
database management and on-line transaction
processing.

As a standard, DCE is being implemented in locations that not only have UNIX experience but also have
experience with IBM. Most of the applications shipping
for DCE have had to place high demands on in-house
UNIX and network administration, and C and C++

programming. They often also require an ability to program in the X Window System, MOTIF, and for connectivity's sake, Microsoft Windows. However, OEC has developed a set of tools that greatly enhances the productivity of developers in DCE environments and in many cases eliminates the need for developers to bother about the details of the above technologies. Also, the OEC tools have taken proprietary non-DCE products, such as Toolbook and Visual Basic, and integrated them into a DCE environment.

A primary feature of OEC is that it makes non-compliant software able to take advantage of DCE/CORBA. On the client devices, OEC libraries adapt graphical user interface (GUI) screen builders for Microsoft Windows, OS/2, Macintosh System 7, and MOTIF to the DCE standard. On the server devices, OEC libraries adapt database engines, including Oracle, Sybase, Informix, Ingress, and Allbase. OEC servers provide a link into the databases of IMS and DB2 for IBM mainframes, and DMS1100 and DMS2 for Unisys mainframes.

Despite its potentially easy programming interface, programmers will still have to understand the fundamentals of their operating system and the science of "make" files. Today, even the leading programmer's development environments have not begun to embrace the idea of replacing the traditional "make" process with object-oriented techniques.

Code Generation and Application Development Services

In CORBA and DCE, all servers consist of four modules: a server stub, a client stub, a definition file, and a procedure file. These modules contain all of the low-level utilities that ensure proper communication between the client and server while the RPC is issued and a return is accepted. Such modules are quite difficult to write and can represent many pages of low-level C code.

OEC application development tools shield developers from this environment by providing services that generate the necessary stub and procedure code for both the client and the server. OEC also allows developers to create robust functionality servers for SQL, a commonly-used database access language. As a development environment, OEC contains all of the necessary testing and debugging suites to ensure that all the code generated and written for your application is in sync.

Application Management Services

At first, the management of a distributed, 3-tiered client-server application sounds like a nightmare: Pieces of code are spread out across different machines, written in many different programming languages. OEC allows system administrators and application developers to automate many of the functions that must be performed to manage such applications.

For example, the NetMinder utility can be configured to monitor the servers of an application to make sure they are up and running. If they are not, the utility will automatically restart them. This same utility can determine if the response time for a particular functionality server is appropriate; if the server is too slow, then NetMinder will start another instance of that server. Version control for transaction processing, security, and other administrative servers have also been implemented as part of the OEC architecture.

Connectivity and Database Servers

There are three ways to access or update data:

1. SQL provides direct access to the database. While SQL is typically used for relational databases, there are translators such as EDA/SQL that can access non-relational data such as IMS and VSAM files.

2. Peer-to-peer servers allow a server program to invoke transactions, including CICS transactions, on a remote machine connected via a peer-to-peer link such as LU6.2, DECnet, or TCP/IP.

3. Terminal emulation or screen-scraping servers access data by emulating a terminal and acting as a user on a remote machine.

OEC tools generate servers that can access or update data using any of these three methods.

OEC: Tools for Every Tier

The 3-tiered client-server architecture has three logical layers, or tiers:

- Presentation (or user interface).

- Functionality, connectivity, and database servers.

- Data. This tier may include existing systems and applications that have been encapsulated to take advantage of this architecture with a minimum of transitional programming effort.

OEC tools support each tier.

OEC Presentation Tier Toolkits

The OEC Presentation Toolkits consist of tools and utilities that reside on the client device and allow screen-building applications to issue remote procedure calls to access data or perform processing. OEC Presentation Toolkits are available for DOS, Microsoft Windows, Macintosh, OS/2, and X/MOTIF. Within these environments GUIs such as Powerbuilder, SQL_Windows, SQL_Forms, Visual Basic, OEC C++, Microsoft, Borland C and C++, Hypercard, Supercard, and many others can utilize the benefits of attaching to the middle or "functionality" tier.

OEC Functionality Tier Toolkits

The toolkits for this tier allow clients and servers to interact across multiple hardware and software environments. At the heart of the OEC functionality tier is the Basic OEC Toolkit. It enables user interfaces to access any data or perform processing through remote procedure calls (RPC). It consists of developer tools as well as RPC servers.

The Basic OEC Toolkit

The Basic OEC Toolkit is currently available for all versions of UNIX (AIX, OSF/1, HP/UX, Ultrix, Solaris, SunOS, SV5). It is also available on VMS, MPE, and OS/2, and will be available soon on MVS and AS/400. The toolkit's components include:

- *OEC Broker*: A naming service that transparently supplies clients with the names and network locations of servers. The Broker also provides security by limiting clients' access to restricted servers. Brokers may run in a hierarchy to create geographical and/or logical domains among an application's servers.

- *RPC Make*: A code generation tool that creates the communication routines necessary to integrate a wide range of presentation tools, graphical user interfaces (GUIs), and programming languages into OEC. This tool empowers developers to "open up" proprietary tools and languages. It offers an easy to use, point-and-click graphical interface.

- *RPC Test*: A debugging utility that allows developers to test servers interactively. Developers choose an RPC by name, specify input values, and immediately see the results of the RPC. Since each server and each RPC can be tested individually, RPC Test minimizes the time and effort needed to fix bugs.

- *RPC Debug*: A graphical interface that provides point-and-click access to the debugging services offered by RPC Test.

- *NetMinder*: A graphical network management tool. Developers and systems administrators can use NetMinder to start the broker-server hierarchies within applications, monitor these configurations once they are running, and change the configurations if necessary. NetMinder can also start or kill an instance of a server. These services can be locked against intruders with NetMinder's security features, which also include the encryption of user names and passwords.

OEC Connectivity Toolkits

The rest of the OEC Functionality Toolkits are known as connectivity servers because they allow access to data from a variety of sources—direct access, database management systems, and terminal emulation access to existing systems.

Remote Connectivity Toolkit

The Remote Connectivity Toolkit resides on the functionality tier and provides connectivity and adapter services in addition to code generation and application development services. With this toolkit, a developer can reduce the time needed to create terminal emulation servers.

The toolkit includes three utilities:

- *Controller*: Directs the flow of communication (the "bytestream") from the remote system toward the emulator component, as well as from the emulator to the remote system. It also has the ability to search the bytestream for specific pieces of data.

- *Emulator*: Acts as a filter to translate certain information in the bytestream. It translates the "escape sequences," those unseen characters in a bytestream that contain formatting information, into code that is understood by the developer's terminal.

- *Scripter*: Offers a high-level development interface that speeds the process of creating terminal emulation servers. A developer need only "script" into the remote system once with scripter watching. As it watches, scripter translates the developer's actions into C code. This C code can then be turned into a server that "scripts" into the remote system by itself.

Open3270 Connectivity Toolkit

The Open3270 Connectivity Toolkit resides on the functionality tier and provides connectivity and adapter services as well as code generation and application development services. With this toolkit, developers can create terminal emulation servers that access IBM's mainframes over an SNA network.

The toolkit includes two utilities:

- *tn3270*: Enables direct terminal access to SNA mainframe applications. It also provides modular programming interfaces that developers can use to automate communication with remote systems. OEC's tn3270 allows concurrent access to both the end-user interface and the programmer's interface, making the results of a developer's actions visible immediately.

- *Genscript*: Creates a scripting interface to SNA mainframes that speeds the process of creating terminal emulation servers by offering a scripting vocabulary and recording the actions of the programmer. Genscript translates those recorded actions into C code, which can then be turned into a terminal emulation server.

Database Connectivity Toolkit

The Database Connectivity Toolkit resides on the functionality tier and provides connectivity and adapter services in addition to code generation and application development services. This toolkit enables developers to build servers that access and manipulate relational database management systems.

The toolkit includes two utilities:

- *SQL Make*: A code generation tool that turns standard ANSI SQL database queries into a database server capable of executing the queries on demand. Servers created with SQL Make can access major relational and non-relational database management systems.

- *A DBMS-specific startup utility*. This might be, for example, the Database Connectivity Toolkit for Informix, which contains SQL Make and IFX Start.

To create a database server, a developer need only write SQL database queries in a format that is specific to the OEC. SQL Make and the startup utility combine to generate the rest of the server code.

Advanced Database Connectivity Toolkit

The Advanced Database Connectivity Toolkit resides on the functionality tier and provides connectivity and adapter services in addition to code generation and application development services. This toolkit allows developers to create servers that implement transaction processing services within the Open Environment Corporation. These servers provide commit and abort capabilities for a variety of relational databases, guaranteeing data integrity during data manipulation.

The toolkit includes the TP Make utility. In order to make a transaction processing server, a developer writes a resource file and an SQL query file. Using these two files, TP Make generates the rest of the server code.

Appendix B
Traditional Architectures

Implementing a client-server architecture in your organization is likely to be a radical proposal; it runs contrary to time-honored (and now outdated) thinking. Beware the lure of vendors seeking to seduce you into the old architectures. In particular, beware of vendors selling a "client-server" architecture comprising only two tiers or built with proprietary tools. They will lock you into their proprietary solutions!

You have identified a strategic information technology application. Now it is time to implement it. Unless the application is unusually simple, the developers will ask for millions of dollars and several years to complete it. Some computer manufacturers may agree and suggest that additional computers are also needed. Some software vendors will promote state-of-the-art application development tools, promising that these tools will cut development time from three years to a year-and-a-half, but only if your technical people buy their proprietary tools.

This appendix discusses two techniques that in general are difficult for implementing your strategic applications. Chances are good that you will recognize them from your own applications:

- Using traditional mainframe environments

- Using a 2-tiered client-server architecture

One final remark on implementing strategic information technology: As with most things in life, there are pretenders. In the world of open systems, pretenders are often products that emulate one or several components in the 3-tiered mix. So be careful—only 3-tiered, client-server, DCE architectures are permissible.

Traditional Mainframe Environments

To appreciate fully the revolutionary nature of the 3-tiered client-server architecture and to determine where your mainframes fit within it, let's examine your current mainframe systems. They have, no doubt, served you reasonably well for many years, and possess specific benefits that you must protect and leverage. However, they also suffer from severe limitations when faced with the problems of today's business environment. The following pages show you why.

But first, a story. This year, the management of a major U.S. bank set out to increase the bank's market share in the metropolitan area from 9% to 20% over a nine-month period. To that end, management identified two critical success factors: acquiring competing banks and increasing customer satisfaction. The second factor seemed to fall out naturally from the first because customers could reasonably be expected to enjoy a greater number of branches.

Then the bank's technical team dropped a bombshell: it could take years to integrate the bank's computer systems with those of its acquisitions. A customer walking into a newly acquired branch to cash a check would have to be turned away; the teller would not be able to access that customer's account information. If the bank could not find a way to integrate the system quickly, its acquisition strategy might actually hurt customer satisfaction. Information technology had suddenly become highly strategic.

But, before we examine client-server architecture, let's look at a classic and prevalent computing system and how that system affects a company.

The Mainframe Architecture

For nearly three decades, the mainframe architecture (and its offspring) has been the computing backbone of businesses around the world. The mainframe architecture offers pluses: stability, security, support, and application base. But of course it also has its minuses: resistance to change, complexity, and cost. First, the advantages:

- *Stability*. It is a well-known and well-understood architecture. It is predictable; you always know exactly what you're getting.

- *Security*. The architecture supports high levels of data security and integrity.

- *Support*. IBM's technical support is legendary. There are armies of senior, highly experienced programmers available to maintain applications.

- *Application base*. Thousands of high volume, stable software applications exist to support all phases and types of business activity. These applications enable smooth communications within and between companies.

And yet, this architecture suffers from equally profound limitations:

- *Resistance to change.* The software infrastructure was originally designed for a class of computer application that was tactical and stable.

- *Complexity.* The software architecture comprises at least half a dozen layers, all of which require careful maintenance (by personnel with highly specialized skills) and present formidable programming challenges when changes are made. This leads to long development times, great difficulty in implementing changes, and technical support that focuses on technology rather than on users' concerns.

- *Cost.* The price/performance ratios for open systems hardware have been revolutionized with advanced RISC technology. The increases in performance have been so dazzling that the MIPS benchmark, once held in esteem by many computer scientists, has fallen by the wayside. It is still meaningful in the present context, however, because it allows us to compare the old with the new. For example, when IBM introduced the model 3090J, it was rated at $90,000/MIP. Today, you can get workstations from DEC, IBM, and HP in the $40 to $75 per MIP range.

The Mainframe Application Environment

Now is the point where we demonstrate the complexity of the traditional computing environment. If this material is unfamiliar or confusing, please bear with us.

168

Let's use the case of Corning Glass. Their application environment looks like this:

Inventory	Order Entry	Inventory (Test Version)	Order Entry (Test Version)	TSO	Payroll (Batch)		
CICS-1		CICS-2				Billing	Market Studies
SNA/VTAM							
OS/VMS						VSE	UNIX
VM							
SNA/NCP/(FEP)							

```
    |          |              IBM 3081              |
  3278      Leased        Corning Corp. HQ        Leased
Terminal     Line          (Corning, NY)           Line
    |                                                |
```

			Materials - Track
	Inventory		Shop Floor
3278— Terminal	IBM 3033		IBM 4331
	(Green Castle, PA)		(Erwin, NY)

What does all of this mean? Each software layer on the 3081 system at corporate headquarters in Corning, NY has the following functions:

- *CICS* (Customer Information Control System). A software switch between applications (such as "Inventory" and "Order Entry" in the illustration). CICS is parameterized to specific applications. The system must be brought down when major changes are made to an application. Consequently, most applications are developed with their own, separate CICS so that changes can be tested without affecting production systems.

- *SNA/VTAM* (System Network Architecture/Virtual Terminal Access Method). A

169

software switch between CICSs. VTAM directs
a transaction to the appropriate CICS.

- *OS/MVS* (Operating System/Multiple Virtual
  Storage). A software switch between jobs. OS
  directs a transaction to the appropriate job.

- *VM* (Virtual Machine). A machine simulator.
  This is a software switch between virtual machines, which are simulated 370s. Several operating systems can run on the same physical
  machine.

- *NCP* (Network Control Program). A software
  switch between different physical machines.

As you can see, this is a lot of layers . . . and a lot of
complexity! Consider the following fragment of software written to run on such an architecture.

Collectively, there are five programming languages
used: PL/1, CICS, 370 Assembler Code, Job Control
Language, and VTAM File Definition. And these languages are a mix of high level languages and machine
languages. The layers of complexity build quickly.

Note in particular that this fragment contains *only 4
lines of executable application code.* All of the remaining lines represent software to deal with the multiple
layers of the architecture!

Application Code (PL/1 and CICS EXECs)

```
EXEC  CICS SEND MAP ('CP2MAP1')
        MAPSET('CP2MAPS') FROM (MAPAREA)
        ERASE;
EXEC  CICS RECEIVE MAP ('CP2MAP1')
        MAPSET('CP2MAPS') SET (MAP1PTR);

{-----------------------------------------}
{ The next 4 lines are the PL/1 application}
{ code:                                    }
{-----------------------------------------}
MONTHGOAL=YEARGOAL/12;
YTDGOAL=MONTHGOAL*MONTH;
RATIO=YTDATTAIN/YTDFOAL;
IF RATIO >= 1 THEN MSG='CONGRATULATIONS!';
{-----------------------------------------}

EXEC  CICS SEND MAP('CP2MAP2')
        MAPSET('CP2MAPS') FROM (MAPAREA)
        ERASE;
        .
        .
        .
```

Define Tables (370 Assembler Code)

```
DFHPPT TYPE=ENTRY
        PROGRAM=GOALPLAN
        PGMLANG=PL1
        PGMSTAT=ENABLED
        .
        .
        .
```

MVS Job Control Language (JCL)

```
//COMPILE JOB 'J.DONOVAN'
//COMPPLIEXEC PLIXCL
//PLI.SYSIN DD *
        PL1 SOURCE
//
        .
        .
        .
```

VTAM File Definition

```
DEFINE CLUSTER(
        NAME(AUDIT.CLUSTER)
        VOL(DSK003))
```

```
DATA(
      NAME(AUDIT.DATA)
      CISZ(4096)
      RECORDS(10000))
      .
      .
      .
```

CICS Screen Map Definition

```
CP2MAP1    DFHMSD      TYPE=MAP,LANG=PL1
           DFHMD1      SIZE=(24,80)
           DFHMDF      POS=(1,70),LENGTH=7,
                       ATTRIB=ASKIP,
                       INITIAL='CP2MAP1'
           DFHMDF      POS=(3,1),LENGTH=5,
                       ATTRIB=ASKIP,
                       INITIAL='GOAL:'
YEARGOAL   DFHMDF      POS=(3,7),LENGTH=7,
                       ATTRIB=UNPRO
```

If you're not technically oriented, now do you understand why our bank's technical team said, "No way."?

Now imagine that your business needs have changed slightly, and you need to modify this application. Even simple changes cause modifications to ripple outward, through all those layers of software. No wonder it takes so many people so many months to implement even the smallest changes; no wonder those changes require so much testing and are so susceptible to bugs and errors. Programming productivity gains are difficult to achieve with this architecture.

Again, the mainframe may be suitable for tactical, stable applications or for larger databases, but for constantly changing applications it provides a difficult environment.

Using traditional methods, hardware, and software made the task of quickly changing systems impossible—at least in our lifetime—and that's only if time stands still. And now you can also see why Blue

Cross/Blue Shield scrapped system 21, even with millions spent.

You need something better.

What You Should Do with Your Mainframes

Take the following actions to maximize your current mainframe investment:

1. Keep and maintain your existing mainframe systems as servers or data sources within your new 3-tiered client-server architecture.

2. Stop developing new applications for your mainframes, except for stable or large databases.

3. Evaluate a right-sizing strategy for possible migration of appropriate applications off the mainframes and onto open systems.

The Limitations of Two Tiers

The client-server architecture separates various functional pieces of an application into discrete units, allowing changes to be made within those units while other units are shielded. Applications are thus easier to maintain and enhance.

Such compartmentalization is not a new idea; vendors have long recognized the limitations of their older architectures and have been seeking to improve them. In fact, the multiple layers of the mainframe architecture which we just examined reflect this impulse to improve matters by introducing new constructs as bridges between earlier layers.

The impulse is good; it is the implementation that has failed.

Indeed, in an effort to jump on the client-server bandwagon, many hardware vendors are promoting software solutions that separate user interfaces and other presentation "clients" from back-end "servers" doing data manipulation and computation. Scrutinize those claims closely. You may discover that such architectures are actually only two tiers deep. You may be separating clients and servers, but both components must run on that single vendor's hardware. Choose this strategy, and you will find yourself locked into the same proprietary structure that now plagues your business.

In this respect, you should be able to see one of the most important dimensions of the 3-tiered solution: It allows an organization to manage its hardware and software suppliers and choose the best products for a given strategic application. One day a computer historian will look back at the older architectures and be baffled at how organizations ever accomplished anything.

Demand that the solution embrace the full three tiers using DCE remote procedure calls, as defined by vendor-neutral standards bodies such as the Open Software Foundation.

Glossary

Terms printed in **bold** in the following definitions are defined elsewhere in this glossary.

3090

An IBM mainframe.

AIX

IBM's implementation of UNIX.

ALPHA

DEC's high-performance computing architecture.

API

Application Programming Interface. The list of functions that define how to access a product.

AS400

Application System 400. An IBM minicomputer.

ATLAS

RPC-based standard for distributed applications defined by UNIX.

Broker

OEC's naming server. A program that acts as a directory, providing **client** programs with the location of **server** programs.

CICS

Customer Information Control System. An IBM subsystem that interfaces between terminal users and host applications.

CISC

Complex Instruction Set Computing. Older hardware architecture, as opposed to **RISC**.

Client
> A program that requests services from external programs, such as **servers,** that may or may not be located on the same physical machine.

CORBA
> Common Object Request Broker. A standard for an open, object-distributed computing environment.

COSI
> Cooperative Open Software Environment. DBMS Database Management System. Software that creates and manipulates data on behalf of external users or programs (for example, **IMS,** HP's Image).

DCE
> Distributed Computing Environment. **RPC**-based standard for distributed applications defined by **OSF.**

DME
> Distributed Management Environment. A set of services for managing applications in **DCE.**

DOS
> Disk Operating System. An operating system for PCs.

ENCINA
> **OLTP** services by Transarc for **DCE.**

GUI
> Graphical User Interface. The style of interface popularized by Macintosh and used in Windows and **MOTIF.**

HP/UX
> Hewlett Packard's implementation of UNIX.

IDL
> Interface Definition Language. A high-level language in which a developer defines how programs interact with each other.

IMS

A database package that runs on IBM mainframes and that internally stores information in a "hierarchical" fashion.

ISO

International Standards Organization. A standards committee based in Europe.

Kerberos

Sophisticated and very safe security protocol developed at MIT and incorporated into **DCE**.

LAN

Local Area Network. A decentralized, small cluster of interconnected computers.

LU6.2

Logical Unit 6.2., a protocol within **SNA** that defines how two computer programs can talk to each other.

MIPS

Million instructions per second. A processor-performance benchmark.

MOTIF

A graphical interface standard defined by **OSF**.

MPE

A Hewlett Packard operating system

MVS

Multiple Vertical Storage. An IBM mainframe operating system.

Naming Service

Service in a distributed environment that provides a **client** program with the location of the **server** programs it needs.

NCP

Network Control Program. A program that manages the top of an **SNA** domain, usually the mainframe.

NetMinder

OEC management service for distributed applications.

NFS

Network File System. Allows the users of one computer to use the disk of another computer as if it were part of their local machine.

OEC

Open Environment Corporation. An open systems vendor and education center providing tools and training to help organizations realize strategic gains from emerging distributed technologies.

OLTP

On-line transaction processing.

Open VMS

A version of **VMS** that complies with open system standards.

OS

Operating System. The software that controls a computer's devices.

OS/2

IBM's graphical operating system for PCs.

OSF

Open Software Foundation. A consortium of vendors who are developing standards for open systems; sponsored by IBM, DEC, HP, et al.

POSIX

API standards defined by the Institute of Electrical and Electronic Engineers; applies to the operating system level to guarantee that a program will be portable from one operating system to another.

RDBMS
> Relational Database Management System. Application to manipulate data structured in interrelated, dynamically created tables, such as Informix, DB2, Oracle, and Ingres.

RISC
> Reduced Instruction Set Computing. Newer processor architecture with smaller, faster instruction sets.

RPC
> Remote Procedure Call. A function that is run on a remote process, typically a different machine.

Server
> A program that performs a set of services for external programs, such as **clients**, which may or may not be located on the same physical machine.

SNA
> Systems Network Architecture. Software that allows a computer to switch between applications; built on a network protocol and architecture, and hardware architecture of the same name.

SOLARIS
> Sun Microsystem's implementation of UNIX.

SQL
> Structured Query Language. A common language for high-level access to relational databases. (See **RDBMS**.)

TCP/IP
> Transmission Control Protocol/Internet Protocol. A standard suite of protocols for sending information across heterogeneous networks.

TUXEDO
> **OLTP** services for **ATLAS**.

ULTRIX
> DEC's implementation of UNIX.

VM

Virtual Machine. An IBM operating system that multiplexes a physical machine into virtual machines that replicate the physical machine's interface; this insulates each user from the effects of other users' programs.

VMS
A DEC proprietary operating system.

VSE
An IBM proprietary mainframe operating system.

VTAM
Virtual Telecommunications Access Method. A program that manages remote access to a mainframe.

WAN
Wide Area Network. A large network, possibly worldwide, composed of several connect **LAN**s.

Windows
A graphical operating system for PCs that runs on top of **DOS**.

Additional Readings

Allison, Graham T. *Window of Opportunity*. New York: Pantheon Books, 1991.

— *Rethinking America's Security: Beyond Cold War to a New World Order*. (edited with Gregory F. Treverton) New York: W.W. Norton and Company, 1992.

—*Essence of Decision: Explaining the Cuban Missile Crisis*. Boston: Little Brown, 1971.

Angle, H. and A. Van de Ven. "Suggestions for Managing the Innovation Journey," Chapter 21 in A. Van de Van, H. Angle, and M.S. Poole, *Research on the Management of Innovation, Volume II*, Cambridge, MA: Ballinger, 1989.

Austin, Nancy and Tom Peters. *A Passion for Excellence*. New York: Random House, 1985.

Brand, Stewart. *The Media Lab: Inventing the Future at MIT*. New York: Viking Press, 1987.

Carnesale, Albert, Graham Allison and Joseph Nye. *Fateful Visions: Avoiding Nuclear Catastrophe*. Cambridge, MA: Ballinger Publishing Company, 1988.

Cohen, Andrew. *You Can Negotiate Anything*. Citadel Press.

Covey, Stephen R. *The Seven Habits of Highly Effective People: Restoring the Character Ethic*. New York: Simon and Schuster, 1989.

Davis, Randall and Douglas B. Lenat. *Knowledge Based Systems in Artificial Intelligence*. New York: McGraw-Hill, 1982.

Donovan, John J. *Opportunities in Technology: Strategic Weapons and Tactics for Executives*. Cambridge, MA: Cambridge Technology Group, 1991.

—"Beyond Chief Information Officer to Network Manager," in *Harvard Business Review* (66:5). Cambridge, MA: Harvard University, 1988.

Drucker, Peter F. *The Practice of Management.* New York: Harper & Row, 1989.

Dunphy, Ed. *The UNIX Industry.* Boston, MA: QED Technical Publishing Group, 1991.

Fineberg, Harvey and Milton Weinstein. *Clinical Decision Analysis.* New York: Saunders Publishing.

Fisher, Roger. *Getting to Yes: Negotiating Agreement Without Giving In.* New York: Viking/Penguin, 1983.

Franko, Lawrence G., "Global Corporate Competition: Who's Winning, Who's Losing, and the R&D Factor as One Reason Why," *Strategic Management Journal,* Vol. 10, 1989, pp. 449-474.

Fried, Charles. *Order and Law: Arguing the Reagan Revolution.* New York: Simon & Schuster, 1991.

Gilbert, X. and P. Strebel, "Developing Competitive Advantage," in *The Strategy Process,* Quinn H. Wintzberg and R. James. Englewood Cliffs, NJ: Prentice Hall, 1988.

Grinyer, P., S. Al-Bazzaz, and M. Yasai-Ardekani, "Towards a Contingency Theory of Corporate Planning: Findings in 48 U.K. Companies," *Strategic Managment Journal,* January-Februrary 1986, pp. 3-28.

Gwertzman, B. *Decline and Fall of the Soviet Empire.* Random House, August 1992.

Hogan, William and Bijan Mossavar-Rahmani et al. *Lower Oil Prices: Mapping the Impact.* Cambridge, MA: Harvard University Energy and Environmental Policy Center, 1988.

Kennedy, Paul. *The Rise and Fall of the Great Powers: Economic Change and Military Conflict from 1500 to 2000.* New York: Random House, 1987.

Kriegel, R. *If It Ain't Broke, Break It.* New York: Warner Books, 1992.

Levitt, Theodore. *The Marketing Imagination.* New York: The Free Press, 1986.

McFarlan, F. Warren and James McKenney. *Corporate Information Systems Management: The Issues Facing Senior Executives.* Homewood, IL: Richard D. Irwin, Inc., 1983.

Madnick, Stuart E. and John J. Donovan. *Operating Systems.* New York: McGraw-Hill, 1974.

Miller and Heiman. *Strategic Selling.* Miller Heiman and Associates.

Morrison, Dr. David. "Change Management in Information Systems," *I/S Analyzer.* Rockville, MD: United Communications Group, 28:8, August, 1990.

Nolan, Richard L. *Managing the Data Resource Function.* St. Paul, MN: West Publishing Company, 1982.

Peck, M. J. "The Japanese Large Corporation: How Different and in What Ways Superior," Yale Working Paper, December 21, 1987.

Phillips, Kevin. *The Politics of the Rich and Poor.* New York: Random House, 1990.

Porter, Michael E. *Competitive Advantage of Their Nation and Their Firm.* New York: The Free Press, 1990.

—*Competitive Advantage.* New York: The Free Press, 1990.

—*Competitive Strategy.* New York: The Free Press, 1985.

Porter, M. "How Competitive Forces Shape Strategy" and "Generic Competitive Strategies," in *The Strategy Process,* Quinn H. Wintzberg and R. James. Englewood Cliffs, NJ: Prentice Hall, 1988.

President and Fellows, Harvard University. *The State of Strategy*, articles from the *Harvard Business Review,* 1985-1991. Boston, MA: Harvard Business School Publishing Division, 1991.

Primozic, Edward, Kenneth Primozic and Joe Laben. *Strategic Choices: Supremacy, Survival or Sayonara.* New York: McGraw Hill, 1992.

Reich, Robert. *The Work of Nations.* New York: Alfred A. Knopf, 1991.

Rockart, John F. and David W. DeLong. *Executive Support Systems, The Emergence of Top Management Computer Use.* Homewood, IL: Dow Jones-Irwin, 1988.

Servan-Schreiber, Jean-Jacques. *The World Challenge.* New York: Simon and Schuster, 1980.

Speller, Jeffrey. *Executives in Crisis.* San Francisco: McMillan, 1989.

Williams, Shirley jointly with Andrew Pierre. *Unemployment and Growth in the Western Economies.* New York: New York University Press, 1985.

Index